INTRODUCTION

I rubbed my eyes as I struggled to stay awake. I was a passenger traveling at night on a highway for what seemed like twelve hours. A split second later, a bright light flashed before my eyes, and then a thunderous boom pierced my ears. It quickly became clear that I was in the middle of an attack.

This wasn't uncommon in Iraq, and I had spent weeks traveling up and down this highway, so it was a matter of time before something violent happened. After the enemy bomb detonated, an eerie silence filled the air. The radio next to me was functioning, but oddly, there was no communication. As my vehicle continued to accelerate through the dense smoke, I noticed the silhouettes of four American soldiers. The bodies were lying on the road, and limbs were moving. I quickly grabbed the radio mic and said, "Bodies on the ground, I'm dismounting."

Within several seconds, gunfire rang out above me, and I cautiously made my way to the first body on the ground.

As I approached the body, his hand reached toward me, and he weakly muttered the word "help." I grasped his hand and noticed the rank of Colonel on his chest. He was the highest-ranking officer of the mission and the main person we were responsible for protecting. I led him to the medic as the other soldiers started to scream and groan in the background. He initially physically resisted me and was determined to assist the other soldiers on the ground, but I convinced him to seek medical treatment first.

The rest of the night was filled with pain, regret, and sorrow. Once all medical treatment was administered, I found myself staring blankly at the horizon, watching the sun slowly rise over the city of Mosul, Iraq. It was difficult to wake up the next day and continue going on endless missions, wondering about my friends who had been injured and fellow soldiers who had died, but I kept doing it. Every single mission was filled with uncertainty and the possibility of another violent attack. What kept me going was a checklist of actions I needed to complete, and systemically I checked them off.

After I completed my deployment, I would return back to Iraq and participate in at least a hundred more combat missions. My salary as an enlisted soldier at the time was around $50,000 a year, and there were no performance bonuses. The only reward for good work was more work and maybe an additional medal to hang from your chest.

As I finished my 20-year military career, I thought deeply about my next job or career. I considered the idea of a federal government job, and it immediately captured my interest. I heard that the federal government valued military veterans, that it was a way to continue serving the country, and that it was a safe and predictable work environment. The federal government offered job stability and benefits that could not be found in the private sector, such as a retirement pension.

What I didn't know is that the entire federal hiring process is confusing, and I often felt like a toddler wandering around in a smoky mirror maze. How did I know what I was qualified for? Why was the process so difficult? Did they actively want to prevent people from applying? There was nothing about getting a federal government job that made sense to me. Why did the federal resume have to be so long? Why does the entire hiring process take six months? Why did I have to apply if I already served twenty years in the military? All of these questions and more were constantly swimming through my mind, and despite searching, I could not find very many answers.

In this book, you will get the answers to those questions and more. This is the information that I wish I had had when considering a federal government job. You will get honesty and transparency in one of the most confusing hiring processes. I will give you these answers as a person who has gone through it multiple times and as a person who has had the privilege of assisting thousands of people attain the same goal you might have, to attain a meaningful, purpose-driven, and well-paid government career. Let's get started.

WHY EVEN TRY?

Many people do not realize that working for the federal government is a realistic option. Instead, people tend to gravitate toward retail jobs, sales jobs, or trying to apply to the latest technology companies. This is because everyone has seen or has heard about the big common companies, and it's familiar. But if you do not personally know anyone who has worked within the federal government, then the thought probably has never crossed your mind.

The federal government has over 2,000,000 employees in over 400 federal agencies across the country and in foreign countries all around the world. This number has been consistent over the past two decades. Literally, every single state in our country has federal job opportunities, even the tiny and rural states. But why would government employment be worth your attention and effort? There are five great reasons why I think that you should consider a federal government job: 1. Stability, 2. Benefits, 3. Pay, 4. Flexibility, and 5. Professional Growth.

STABILITY

In your lifetime, there will probably be recessions, wars, and plenty of economic uncertainty. The labor market will react based on what is happening around the world. The one employer that has the highest probability of security and stability is the federal government. As long as the United States exists, it will need federal government employees. This can shield you from company bankruptcies, layoffs, or organizational restructuring that is more common in the private sector.

Being fired or terminated from your job due to a personality conflict or other trivial issue is significantly reduced. You are a lot less likely to experience age discrimination. After completing a short probationary period, you are typically not considered an "at-will" employee anymore. You will have rights and protections as an employee. This means nobody can fire you at a whim for just about any reason. There will be due process and an appeal process with union protections. These protections can reduce your stress and anxiety.

BENEFITS

There are over a dozen benefits in the federal government. This includes healthcare, life insurance, a thrift savings plan, work/life balance, gym access, and telework opportunities. But the best one by far has to be the federal pension. A pension is guaranteed money you will receive for the rest of your life. The pension amount could easily be over $3,000 a month, depending on how long you have worked for the government and the highest salary you were able to attain. This is not money invested in the stock market; it's not associated with a social security check, and it's not money that is dependent on any type of investment. The federal pension is guaranteed by the U.S. government, and as long as the United States exists, the federal pension will be there. The federal pension alone could easily be worth over a million dollars, and it provides a true sense of financial security during uncertain times. The pension is the main reason why people are willing to take a pay cut late in their careers just to secure an additional stream of income. The most common ages at which you can start collecting your pension are usually at age 57, 60, or 62, but there are some situations in which you can earn it even earlier.

PAY

You are probably not paid enough. Most people in the country do not have a decent salary. The average salary in the U.S. right now is $59,384, which is about $28 an hour. Many people have been conditioned to think that a wage of $15 to $20 an hour is somehow acceptable, but that type of money is not going to be enough for you to reach your goals. It's not enough to raise and provide for a family or to be able to afford a house. By comparison, the average federal government salary is around $100,000 a year, and your salary can exceed $200,000 for certain types of government jobs.

On top of your annual salary in a government job, there are opportunities to get annual and semi-annual performance bonuses, overtime pay, locality pay, and quality step increases that can suddenly increase your salary by thousands of dollars. And if your current salary isn't enough, in a federal government job, you are usually able to apply for a promotion every twelve months. A common misconception of government pay is that it's too low or undesirable, and for many of us, that's not true.

If you are earning over $200,000 a year right now, then perhaps the pay aspect of government jobs might not be that attractive. Instead, it could be another benefit or the call of public service that has you interested in a government job. But if you are a part of the millions of workers currently earning minimum wage in the U.S. or if you are hovering below the average salary in this country in a dead-end job, then the pay will be highly attractive.

FLEXIBILITY

How would you like to work while sitting comfortably on your coach or next to the kitchen table? Telework and remote work options make it a reality, and it's available in many federal government jobs. Thousands of federal employees stay at home each day and work on their laptop computers. There is no sitting in a traffic jam for over an hour or a tedious morning commute. This means that you can put a load of laundry in or start a dishwasher cycle during your 15-minute break. You can heat up a quick snack in your microwave. You can also save a lot of money on expensive car maintenance, fuel costs, and parking costs and save the most precious resource of all, your time.

You can always try to make more money throughout your life, but regardless of your talents and skills, you will never be able to create more minutes or hours. Your time is precious when you are pursuing your goals and dreams, and time passes by too fast. Our children are only little for a small window of time; they look up to you, and those moments are priceless. However, many private sector jobs will completely drain you of all your time and then dispose of you when times become inconvenient. Ask yourself, what will happen when you stop working? Who is there for you? The answer is probably your friends and family. Shouldn't you invest more time in those relationships? In a federal government job, work-life balance is a reality.

PROFESSIONAL GROWTH

It is frustrating and mind-numbing to be stuck in a dead-end job as you watch your life slowly pass by. For example, many people get into retail jobs or security jobs with the idea of it being a temporary situation, and then months turn to years or decades, and then one day, you are waking up in your bed in your forties, and you wonder where it all went wrong. You need some potential for growth to be built into your job, or you will not be satisfied for long in your position.

Regardless of what day or time it is, there are over 10,000 open federal governments around the world on USAJob.gov. This includes hundreds of jobs in foreign countries such as Spain, Italy, Japan, and Germany. The best part of growth in a government job is that you are eligible for a promotion after just twelve months. You could rapidly move up through the pay scale every year if you had the desire. Not only would your pay dramatically increase, but a lot of times, your duties and responsibilities would change. This gives you the development and growth you need.

You will still see plenty of government employees who refuse to apply for any promotions, and they seem content in their positions. Some people are happy spending 30+ years in the same federal agency, but the choice to move up, challenge yourself, and earn more pay will always be there. It is rare to work in an organization that has the potential for unlimited mobility; you can jump around from state to state or country to country while continuing to grow in your federal career.

Take Action:

Create a USAJobs.gov account today

HIRING PREFERENCES

There are a lot of different hiring preferences recognized by the federal government, but you do not need any of them to get a government job. Many people get discouraged when they learn just how many hiring paths exist, and many times, they do not qualify for any of the special hiring paths. The first screen you see when applying to a federal government job announcement is the "eligibility assessment" section, which usually consists of around fifteen questions that you will probably answer "No" to, and that could make you question the hiring process.

However, there is a way you do not have to compete with all the hiring paths, and that is by applying for jobs under the direct hiring authority (DHA). DHA is granted to federal agencies that have proved a critical hiring need or if a severe shortage of qualified candidates exists. You can type in "direct hire" or "DHA" into the keyword search bar in USAJobs.gov and click "search" to start searching for job announcements using the direct hire authority. If you have never been a federal government employee, then you will most likely be applying for "Open to Public" job announcements. If you have any other hiring paths available to you, then you need to ensure that they are selected in your USAJobs filters.

Another way to bypass hiring preferences is by attending federal hiring events both in person and virtually so that you can connect with real human beings, such as a human resource specialist, hiring coordinator, or hiring manager. Most of the federal government hiring events are announced on USAJobs.gov, but some of them can only be found on an agency's website. These potential relationships you can make can end up making the difference when it comes to you getting a government job. I have witnessed people get a high-salary job offer without applying to USAJobs.gov by leveraging relationships they made while attending federal government hiring events.

If you have held a job for at least a few years, you probably have the right background and experience for a government job. I have witnessed and helped hundreds of people of all types of backgrounds successfully accept a government job offer. This also includes people who have never held a paying job and were able to use their volunteering experience to meet the qualifications of the job announcement. Unlike the private sector, the federal government fully acknowledges your experience, even if it is not paid experience. Do not think you need to have a certain military background, college education, or specific corporate background to be found eligible. You do not; you just need to have a job search focus and be able to explain how your experience is relevant.

Let's go through a few of the most common hiring paths the federal government uses and that you will see on USAJobs.gov:

COMPETITIVE SERVICE

This hiring path is usually for current government employees or eligible military veterans. Competitive Service positions are positions subject to the laws passed by Congress to ensure that applicants and employees receive fair and equal treatment in the hiring process.

In the competitive service, you must go through a competitive hiring process before being appointed, which is open to all applicants. Competitive Service jobs must be advertised publicly, and that's usually on USAJobs.gov.

EXCEPTED SERVICE

Excepted service agencies set their own qualification requirements and are not subject to the appointment, pay, and classification rules in the United States Code. If you enter the government under noncompetitive hiring paths such as with Veterans Recruitment Appointment or Schedule A, then you will likely be under excepted service. Some jobs under the Excepted Service do not need to be on USAJobs.gov. Also, many law enforcement jobs under the Department of Justice or Department of Homeland Security will be under the excepted service.

INTERNAL TO AN AGENCY

You're eligible if you're a current federal employee at the hiring agency that is announcing the job. At times, this will be specific to a certain subagency or particular office within a subagency. Make sure you read the entire job announcement to understand exactly who may apply.

VETERANS

Veterans have two important categories:

1. Veteran Preference and 2. Special Hiring Authorities

Veteran Preference:

0 Point Preference – If you were released or discharged from a period of active duty from the armed forces after August 29, 2008, by reason of being the only surviving child in a family in which the father or mother or one or more siblings.

1. Served in the armed forces, and
2. Was killed, died as a result of wounds, accident, or disease, is in a captured or missing in action status, or is permanently 100 percent disabled or hospitalized on a continuing basis (and is not employed gainfully because of the disability or hospitalization), where
3. The death, status, or disability did not result from the intentional misconduct or willful neglect of the parent or sibling and was not incurred during a period of unauthorized absence.

5 Point Preference – If your active-duty service meets any of the following:

1. For more than 180 consecutive days, other than for training, any part of which occurred during the period beginning September 11, 2001, and ending on August 31, 2010, the last day of Operation Iraqi Freedom, OR
2. During the Gulf War, between August 2, 1990 and January 2, 1992, OR

3. For more than 180 consecutive days, other than for training, any part of which occurred after January 31, 1955, and before October 15, 1976, OR
4. Between April 28, 1952, and July 1, 1955, OR
5. In a war, campaign, or expedition for which a campaign medal or badge has been authorized.

10 Point Preference – If you served in the military at any time and have a service-connected disability or received a Purple Heart.

SPECIAL HIRING AUTHORITIES

<u>Veteran Recruitment Authority</u> (VRA) is an excepted authority that allows an agency to non-competitively appoint an eligible veteran. If you:

- Served during a war or are in receipt of a campaign badge for service in a campaign or expedition; or
- are a disabled veteran or
- are in receipt of an Armed Forces Service Medal (includes the Global War on Terrorism Service Medal) for participation in a military operation or
- are a recently separated veteran (within 3 years of discharge) and
- separated under honorable conditions (this means an honorable or general discharge).

You can be appointed under this authority at any grade level up to and including a General Schedule (GS)-11 or equivalent.

Veterans Employment Opportunities Act (VEOA) – Your latest discharge must be issued under honorable conditions (this means an honorable or general discharge), AND you must be either:

- a preference eligible (defined in title 5 U.S.C. 2108(3)), or
- a veteran who substantially completed 3 or more years of active service under honorable conditions.

30% or More Disabled Veteran authority – You are eligible if you:

- retired from active military service with a service-connected disability rating of 30% or more or
- have a rating by the Department of Veterans Affairs showing a compensable service-connected disability of 30% or more.

MILITARY SPOUSES

Federal agencies can use the military spouse non-competitive hiring process to fill positions on either a temporary or permanent basis. You're eligible if you are:

- A spouse of an active duty member of the armed forces.
- A spouse of a service member who is 100% disabled due to a service-connected injury at the time of separation from military service.
- A spouse of a service member killed while on active duty.

You are no longer eligible if you remarry.

NATIONAL GUARD & RESERVES

- Require you to already be a National Guard member in a specific state.
- Require you to already be a National Guard member, but willing to transfer to a specific state.
- Are open to anyone, but you must join the National Guard to accept the job.
- Require you to wear a National Guard uniform.

STUDENTS & RECENT GRADUATES

Students – The Internship Program is for current university/college students. The Program provides students in high schools, colleges, trade schools, and other qualifying educational institutions with paid opportunities to work in agencies and explore Federal careers while completing their college education.

Recent Graduates - It is to promote possible careers in the civil service to individuals who, within the previous two years, graduated from qualifying educational institutions with an associate's, bachelor's, master's, professional, doctorate, vocational, or technical degree or certificate from qualifying educational institutions. To be eligible, applicants must apply within the previous two years of degree or certificate completion, except for veterans precluded from doing so due to their military service obligation, who will have up to six years after degree or certificate completion to apply.

INDIVIDUALS WITH DISABILITIES

This path is for Schedule A, which refers to a special hiring authority that gives federal agencies an optional and potentially quicker way to hire individuals with disabilities. Applying under Schedule A offers an exception to the traditional competitive hiring process. You can apply for jobs using Schedule A if you are a person with an intellectual disability, a severe physical disability, or a psychiatric disability.

To be eligible for Schedule A, you must provide proof of a disability letter stating that you have an intellectual disability, severe physical disability, or psychiatric disability. You can get this letter from your doctor, a licensed medical professional, a licensed vocational rehabilitation specialist, or any federal, state, or local agency that issues or provides disability benefits.

PEACE CORPS & AMERICORPS VISTA

You're eligible if your service as a volunteer or volunteer leader totals at least one year with the Peace Corps or one year of service with AmeriCorps VISTA.

Your non-competitive eligibility lasts for one year after completing your Peace Corps or AmeriCorps service. Federal agencies may extend the period for up to three years if, after your completed service, you are:

- In the military service.
- Studying at a recognized institution of higher learning.

- Involved in another activity, which, in the agency's view, warrants an extension.

Keep in mind that none of these hiring paths will ever guarantee you a job. There are no guarantees when it comes to federal government job offers, but there are best practices and ways you can greatly increase the probability of getting a job offer.

Take Action:

Identify your hiring path(s) and set it in your filters on USAJobs.gov.

YOUR NEXT JOB

Speaking of job filters on USAJobs.gov, the filters on that website are everything. Do not try to use a website like the Google search engine. If you are randomly searching for job announcements, you are wasting your time because even if you find one or two opportunities, you are missing the larger picture. Not using filters is also a quick way to become discouraged and quit your job search too early.

You need to search your filters at a minimum by:

- City or Zip Code (25-mile radius)
- Hiring Path
- Job Series
- Salary or General Schedule (GS) grade

After creating your USAJobs.gov account, save those filters and select to be reminded of new jobs on a daily or weekly basis. This will give you a narrow focus on the jobs that match your resume. This needs to be done to save you time and to give you the best chance of getting the job. Also, consider sorting by "close date" because you wouldn't want to miss out on job announcements that could be closing today. But what jobs are you eligible for, or what job do you even want to do?

What should your job in the federal government be? There are hundreds of job series in the federal government, and most people are eligible for multiple job series.

Here are three places where you should start:

1. USAJobs.gov

    On this website, when you click "Series" on the right-hand side of the screen, you can scroll down through over a hundred different job series. Some of the names of these job series will immediately pop out to you because you will notice similarities with your experience and skills. Write down and remember the ones that interest you, and then you can research them more.

2. OPM Job Series Handbook (2018)

    You can find this handbook on OPM.gov or do a Google search and download it. This is where you are researching your potential job series. In this 200+ page handbook, you will find the exact way Human Resources is classifying the job positions. This gives you an insight into what it takes to qualify for a lot of different jobs. Once you open the file, search the document by looking for actions you have experience in. For example, if you have experience analyzing budgets, search for "budget" or "analyze," and then you will be able to determine what job series you might be a good fit for.

3. Talk to Federal Employee

    If you know someone who is working a federal government job in a federal agency, you should talk to them about how they got their job. How can you follow similar steps to get your government job? This is what people call "informational interviews."

Thankfully, with LinkedIn, you can even do this with people you do not know.

Informational interviews or networking is basically a value exchange. They're providing you value by giving you information, and you are providing value, which could be buying them a cup of coffee or tea. Reach out to people that have a similar background, either prior military, similar hometowns, same type of degree, went to the same school, same interests, etc. Ask those people for fifteen minutes of their time either over the phone or in person at a local cafe/restaurant. If you do this correctly, you are building a relationship from which you will benefit for years to come.

If you are an introvert or socially awkward, it is harder to put yourself in a vulnerable situation to reach out to strangers, but it is something that is so valuable you must try, and like exercising a muscle, you will slowly get better at it. At first, start small; maybe try for one informational interview a month and then increase it to one informational interview a week. The more that you communicate and practice building relationships, the easier it will become.

I still remember being nervous when meeting strangers at my local cafe, but the information that was shared with me was incredibly useful, and talking to others was one of the best decisions I made during my transition to federal employment. Talking to just one person can open up a connection to a completely different person who has the influence to make an impact in your job search.

Here are some of the most common job series that people are interested in (keep in mind that there are about three hundred different job series):

0300 General Administrative

This job series covers almost all administrative jobs, and it's one of the largest federal government job series. Almost every federal agency requires a 0300 employee to perform basic administrative functions. If you have experience reviewing documents, writing emails, updating policy letters, working with Excel spreadsheets, or organizing folders, then you probably have the required experience for many of these jobs. These jobs usually have zero educational requirements, and many people who have held retail or office-type jobs have the necessary experience to be eligible for these jobs.

0500 Accounting and Budget

This job series covers multiple finance-type jobs. The three main job series that are usually easier to get into and don't always have educational requirements are the 0501 Financial Administration, 0503 Financial Clerical And Assistance, and 0560 Budget Analyst.

Other finance job series, such as the 0510 Accounting and 0512 Revenue Agent, will have an educational requirement, such as a bachelor's degree with twenty-four accounting semester hours or a Certified Public Accountant certificate.

1100 Business

1101 General Business and 1102 Contracting are the most common jobs in this series, and many of them require a bachelor's degree (in any field) and twenty-four credit hours in business. Usually, people with business college degrees come looking for this job series, and if you do not have any experience, you can expect to start off at a low level, such as GS-6 or GS-7.

A lot of people with business degrees are eager to get into this job series even if they have to start at a lower GS grade, but after a couple of years, they find the work rather stressful, and they look to pivot to another job series.

1700 Education

This series is for instructors, teachers, and curriculum designers, among other educational jobs. You do not always need to have a college education to be qualified for these jobs, but you will need experience. This job series is not solely for teachers or professors. If you have compiled a PowerPoint presentation, presented information to an audience, facilitated practical exercises, or drafted handbooks, then you could have the necessary experience directly relevant to Education jobs. Many people forget about the times they have spent instructing or teaching because it was not a core part of the job; it was an additional duty or something they only did several times, but that experience can still count.

2200 Information Technology Specialist

This is another popular job series because it involves many areas of technology; here are some of the different areas of focus:

- IT Specialist
- Help Desk
- Software Developer
- Enterprise Management
- Information Security
- Cybersecurity
- Artificial Intelligence

Thankfully, more federal agencies are including the specialty in the title of the job announcement so that way you can further focus your search and not click on a job announcement you have no experience with. For example, you can find job announcement titles that are worded as "IT Specialist (INFOSEC)," and if you are targeting information security, you can apply to it.

When applying to federal government jobs on USAJobs.gov, oftentimes, there will be a question asking if you are okay with the agency sharing your application with other offices or agencies. You always want to mark down "yes" to this question. This is a new initiative the federal government has been focusing on called "pooled hiring." It enables agencies to share hiring actions, and it reduces the time and effort the government makes to find qualified candidates. I saw a lady apply for a 0343 government job at the Department of Energy and a month later received an interview request for a 0560 government job at the same agency. She never applied for the 0560 position but still landed the interview. This happens because the agency is retaining and sharing your job application with other offices, and you could be contacted by a hiring manager who is interested in your background.

There are also many financial incentives and relocation incentives that could be included if you are willing to sign a service agreement, which is a document that states you intend to stay with the agency for so many years, and in return, they will give you a lump sum of money. Relocation incentives are usually for existing federal employees, but as a new federal employee, you may qualify for reimbursable relocation expenses. Make sure you get this in writing. Only certain things are reimbursed and at a rate set by the government.

Next, you should understand the three different "services" that federal government jobs can fall into on USAJobs.gov. You will be able to quickly identify the service type by opening a job announcement and looking at the "Overview" column to the right, scrolling down, and reading underneath the word "Service." The different services include:

1. Competitive Service

    Accepting a job under the competitive service will allow you to become a status candidate after three years. Many people refer to this as a type of "tenure," as you can leave your federal government job at any point and then re-enter into the competitive service by applying to jobs on USAJobs.gov.

This gives you an advantage in searching for jobs as the majority of the general public can only apply to "open to the public" jobs, so if you become a "status candidate," then you will potentially have thousands of additional jobs you can apply to on USAJobs.gov that the general public cannot.

2. Excepted Service

    Many information technology jobs in the Department of Defense and federal law enforcement agencies in the Department of Homeland Security and Department of Defense will be under the Excepted Service, and this is because of the way they hire and select their applicants. If the agency has an "interagency agreement," then you can also apply for competitive service jobs. If not, then you will be restricted to "open to the public" and "excepted service" jobs. There is nothing wrong with this, and many people make an entire 30- or 40-year career in the Excepted Service without any issues. It will depend on what your career goals are.

3. Senior Executive

    This is for executive positions that are above GS-15. If you are aiming to become a Senior Executive, it will change the way you are submitting your job application as you will have to meet the five Executive Core Qualifications, including:

    - Leading change
    - Leading people
    - Results driven

- Business acumen
- Building coalitions

There are also government jobs that are politically appointed, including senior executives and Schedule C employees. Most job seekers do not consider this part of the government and would prefer to search on USAJob.gov. If you decide to apply for a politically appointed job, keep in mind that one of the optional fields to fill out is disclosing your political party. You will be instructed to upload your resume and answer questions about your desired function, area of interest, and federal agency.

The downside to these positions is that they are "at-will," meaning you can be terminated easily, and once the administration in the White House changes, your government job could be in jeopardy. If you are interested in bringing your skills and experience to a politically appointed position, you can apply for these types of opportunities outside of the USAJobs.gov website. Visit the website below:

https://www.whitehouse.gov/get-involved/join-us/

Take Action:

Identify the job series you're eligible for and start creating a separate resume for each job series you're interested in.

YOUR SALARY

After you have a job series targeted, the next question is how much does your salary need to be to keep or improve your current lifestyle? Do not fall into the trap of feeling that you need to take a pay cut to "get your foot in the door." You should not have to take a pay cut. Many federal government jobs can pay well into the six figures.

The most common pay scale in the federal government is the GS (General Schedule) pay scale, which covers about 70% of federal government employees. GS grades go from GS-1 to GS-15, and there are 10 steps for each grade. These 10 steps will take a total of 18 years to move through, but there are some ways to accelerate this time. The normal waiting periods between steps are:

- 12 months between steps 1-4
- 24 months between steps 5-7
- 36 months between steps 8-10

You should have a GS grade or salary range in mind before applying, even if you are not applying for GS-grade jobs. Generally, for someone with three to five years of experience, this could be GS-7 to GS-11, or with someone with 10 – 15 years of experience, this could be GS-12 to GS-14. The exact GS grade range will depend on your geographic location, the job series, and how much experience you have. But I would first start looking at the GS Payscale on the OPM website; there are over 50 different pay charts based on locations, and find a salary amount that satisfies your personal requirements.

There are also other pay scales that can have salaries that go even higher than a GS-15, step 10. These pay scales exist in certain agencies and offices within the Veterans Affairs, Federal Aviation Administration, Security Exchange Commission, and Federal Deposit Insurance Corporation, among other federal agencies.

Another common pay band is within the Federal Wage System, which is a pay-setting system that covers employees who are paid by the hour and classified as Wage Grade (WG) employees. WG jobs are also available on USAJobs.gov and will cover mostly trade and labor jobs. There are separate pay scales for WG jobs, and those scales usually display an hourly wage instead of an annual salary. If you do accept a WG job, you can still apply for GS-grade jobs; once again, it will depend on your experience. For some reason, the government still categorizes white collared jobs as GS jobs and blue-collar jobs as WG jobs.

When you receive your federal government job offer, chances are it will probably be given to you at Step 1 level regardless of your GS grade or previous experience. But you can usually negotiate your step level. It's the responsibility of the job applicant to initiate this negotiation; otherwise, it will probably never happen, and you could easily miss out on tens of thousands of dollars. Many people make the mistake of accepting the first job offer at Step 1. But we will go into that a lot more later.

There is a concept called GS Grade inflation that can occur in larger metropolitan cities such as Washington D.C., New York City, and San Francisco, CA. This means that GS grades tend to be higher in bigger cities than in rural areas; this is largely due to the cost of living. It can be hard to compete for talent in an expensive area. So, a person working as a GS-12 in North Dakota could potentially be a Branch Chief in charge of an entire division, and that same GS-12 in Washington D.C. could be an Administrative Specialist without being responsible for anybody except for themselves.

Take Action:

Identify the pay range you're willing to accept. This is typically done by GS grade and can vary greatly by your location.

HORRIBLE RESUME

The number one reason you will not get a federal government job is because of your resume. Without the right resume, you will never get an invitation to an interview or a job offer. It is not enough to be "qualified," that will not normally get you an interview. There are usually four categories your resume and job application can fall into: 1. Not Qualified, 2. Qualified, 3. Well Qualified, and 4. Best Qualified. We need to get you into the "Best Qualified" category, and we can do that with your federal resume. The concept behind your federal resume is simple, but millions of people constantly fail to fix their resume. Here are some reasons why yours could be horrible.

#1 IT DOESN'T GO INTO DETAIL

No assumptions about your experience can ever be made. Please read that again. This means that you have to go into details that you probably do not have to go into when writing a private sector resume. This means that if your job is as an accountant right now, you still have to explain specifically that you know how to review and produce Microsoft Excel spreadsheets or that you know how to use Microsoft Outlook. It can seem silly and unnecessary to put that much information into your federal resume but that is what Human Resources will use to determine how qualified you are and to justify a legal hire or not.

#2 YOU FOCUS ON RESPONSIBILITIES

Just because you were responsible for a task or action does not mean you completed it well. Plenty of people have been responsible for a special project and then performed it to a below-average standard. Instead of responsibilities, focus on your achievements. Here's an example of a common resume bullet that I typically see:

- Served as a coordinator for many tasks in the company

The above bullet might qualify you for the skill of coordination, but it's an incredibly weak bullet. It doesn't mention how you coordinated or what the direct result of the coordination was. Here is a better way to write the bullet:

- Coordinated multiple project meetings through problem-solving, planning, and communication to identify and resolve budget issues

The above bullet is a little better because it talks more about the task that you coordinated, and there's a direct result given for the action, but we can do better than that. Let's try to write it like this instead:

- Coordinated 12 project meetings and used strategic problem-solving, planning, and effective communication to identify and resolve budgetary challenges in Oracle NetSuite. This approach directly contributed to a significant 20% reduction in budget discrepancies. Praised by senior leadership and received a strong performance appraisal.

The above bullet is an example of a strongly worded achievement. It's quantified, provides the proper context, and has two result-oriented outcomes. I would consider the above bullet a step above an "achievement." Instead, I consider it a "success story," and it's an important part of your resume. Include one strongly worded success story for each job position on your resume, and it should be at the top. It's at the top because we want it to be the first thing that people read when reading your resume, and it should be directly relevant to the job series and job announcement you are applying for. Below your success story should be a list of your relevant achievements for each job position.

If you spend a few seconds of your time asking yourself the following questions before typing out your achievements, your results when applying to federal government jobs will improve dramatically. When you start creating your achievements, keep in mind that it should answer the following questions:

- How did you do the action?
- What was the result of the action?
- Can you quantify it?

If your achievement doesn't answer at least two of the three above questions, then it is probably not strong enough, and you should spend more time explaining the details of your achievement. You also need to make the achievement relevant to the job that you are applying to. If you have multiple jobs in your resume with achievements that are not relevant, consider removing those irrelevant achievements and replacing them with something more relevant.

Instead of filling your resume with a list of generic responsibilities, have strongly worded achievements instead. But what if you have forgotten all of your past achievements? In that case, take a look at your past performance reviews, awards, and certificates to recall actions you've taken that are relevant to the job you are targeting.

Another helpful approach to creating your achievement bullets in your resume is to include the following components: Action verbs, skills, impact statements, and impact metrics. Take this achievement bullet, for example:

- Provided support in the budget formulation process by analyzing funding amounts in multiple Excel spreadsheets and creating annual budget templates while increasing the operational compliance rating by 15%.

Let's dissect the components of the achievement from above.

Action verbs: Provided and analyzed

Skills: Budget formulation and Excel spreadsheets,

Impact statement: Increasing the operational compliance rating

Impact metrics: by 15%

It is fine to describe your job responsibilities in the first paragraph, but after that, you should focus on achievements instead of responsibilities. When listing your achievements in your resume, try to have them in order of strength.

#3 IT IS NOT LONG ENOUGH

A one-page federal resume is likely not going to cut it unless you are applying to your first job or you have less than a year of experience. Sure, there will always be those anomalies out there that land a federal job with a one-pager, but it is highly unlikely. You need to go into great detail, so the expectation for your resume is that it will be a few pages long. However, I advise you not to exceed five pages. More federal agencies are starting to cut off their reviews at the five-page mark, which is great because when people submit thirty page resumes (it has happened), it slows down the hiring process for everyone. If you are having a hard time keeping it to five pages, consider only including the last ten years of experience or removing achievements that are not relevant to the job you are applying to.

#4 IT IS NOT RELEVANT

No matter how amazing your achievements are, they mean nothing if your actions are not directly relevant to the job you are applying for. Part of what makes your achievements strong is the fact that they are relevant to the job announcement. If you are applying to be an Instructor, then your stellar achievements in identifying and resolving budget errors as a Budget Analyst might not be relevant and could be dismissed entirely. Think about what you did at your previous jobs and find a way to make your experience relevant to the job announcement you are applying to, even if, on the surface, it might not seem relevant.

For example, volunteering at the local school might not seem like an experience that can help us get a finance position, but maybe you assisted in analyzing fundraiser information and updating spreadsheets based on donation amounts. Maybe you communicated to parents during a book fair, and it increased revenue during that event. We can often glance over some of our past accomplishments that could help us get our next job.

#5 KEY INFORMATION IS MISSING

There is information required in a federal resume that is not required in a typical private sector resume. This includes:

- The job title, starting and ending dates (including month and year), prior employer's name and address
- The average number of hours worked per week in each job position
- Supervisor's name, address, and telephone number; and whether you're most recent supervisor may be contacted
- Any Special Hiring Authorities that are applicable

There are times you can be disqualified by forgetting to include key information. If you have any doubts about what information needs to be in your federal resume, then you should use Resume Builder, which is on the USAJobs.gov website, because it will guide you in inputting the correct information. If you are confident about what should be included in a federal resume, then I would recommend writing your own federal resume on Microsoft Word because you can control a lot more of the styling and format to make the resume easier to read. There are some federal agencies that do not take custom resumes, such as many job announcements the Coast Guard has, and if you want to apply to those government jobs, you must have a resume in the Resume Builder format. Personally, I have both, but the custom one is what I prefer.

Do not worry yourself about any employment gaps you may have in your federal resume. The federal government does not take away points for employment gaps, and you do not need to explain yourself. If you are feeling self-conscious about an employment gap, consider including volunteer experience, such as when you may have volunteered at the local school, church, or city government. You should also include your business if you were or are a business owner. All of your experience counts.

FEDERAL RESUME EXAMPLE

Below is an example of a federal resume that is targeting the 0501 Financial Administration job series. I included it to help you format and style your own resume. It should be used as a template, but you still need to include your own experience and achievements. Notice that below the responsibility paragraph, there is a quantified strong success story. This has been a proven format that gets strong results. Remember that you need to adjust your resume to the exact job announcement that you're applying for, if possible. Some job announcements will use different verbs or require different skills, even if they are in the same job series.

Tracy Duncan

Address: 421 Stormy Road
Phone: (555) 123-4567
Email: Tracyducan123@gmail.com

U.S. Citizen | Schedule A

Relevant Work Experience

Commercial Credit Analyst   05/2017 to Present
Magnify, Richmond, VA   40 hours/week
Supervisor: Rusty Burt, 555-653-5363 (May Contact)   Annual Salary: $95,000

Daily Duties and Responsibilities:

Responsible for analyzing and assessing business clients' financial situation, liabilities, and history to determine their eligibility for credit and at what limit. Analyzed and verified financial statements, credit reports, and economic data to evaluate risk, helping businesses make sound lending choices while safeguarding their financial health.

- *Reduced loan delinquency rates by 20% in 12 months. Conducted in-depth financial analysis and assessment of existing and prospective clients' financial statements and credit histories, which resulted in a 15% increase in the quality of the client portfolio. This contributed to a significant risk mitigation strategy and enhanced the overall financial stability of the organization.*

Resolved financial discrepancies, resulting in a 10% reduction in error-related financial losses and the implementation of recommendations that yielded annual cost savings of $75,000. Delivered financial administration services, contributing to an improvement in process efficiency.

Analyzed financial workflows throughout the budget cycle, ensuring compliance with financial management rules and regulations. Oversight led to a 20% reduction in compliance-related issues, resulting in improved financial accountability and risk mitigation.

Analyzed and evaluated budget acquisition plans and multi-year programs, identifying cost-saving opportunities that translated into a reduction in procurement expenses. This approach enhanced financial stewardship and maximized the efficiency of resource allocation.

Conducted comprehensive risk assessments for potential lines of credit, resulting in an increase in the approval rate of credit applications. The risk assessments facilitated confident lending decisions and contributed to the acquisition of $2 million in new credit lines, increasing the organization's lending portfolio and revenue potential.

Designed and updated briefings and other presentations supporting assigned program reviews and other administrative assessments supporting program goals and priorities. Coordinated strategic sourcing scheduling and planning, project future needs, and critical resource needs.

Financial Analyst   03/2014 – 04/2017
McKesson, Richmond, VA   40 hours/week
Supervisor: Clark Fuente, 555-312-4563 (Contact Me First)   Annual Salary: $85,000

Planned, forecasted, and analyzed revenue and vendor buyside gross profit. Provided financial expertise through analytics, displayed intellectual curiosity, and continuously improved processes and models. Collaborated with business partners across multiple functions and levels and used influence to provide recommendations.

- ***Reduced operational costs by 15%.*** *Conducted cost-benefit analyses of alternative methods for managing the organization's programs and administrative operations. The data-driven approach identified efficiency opportunities and an annual cost savings of $200,000. The recommendations produced from these analyses improved resource allocation and financial sustainability.* ***Received a strong annual performance evaluation.***

Implemented legal and regulatory controls over approved budgets, leading to a 100% compliance rate with financial regulations and a 25% reduction in audit findings. These measures ensured financial transparency and minimized risk.

Analyzed financial data from multiple diverse sources to identify problem trends and develop corrective courses of action. The insights led to a 12% reduction in financial discrepancies across the organization.

Developed executive reporting, financial forecasting, and risks and opportunities assessment, which resulted in a 15% improvement in forecast accuracy. Enabled the identification of revenue opportunities, yielding an increase in annual revenue.

Advised management on effective and efficient methods for acquiring and utilizing funds to support the organization's programs and activities. Implemented recommendations that resulted in an increase in funding acquisition success, securing additional funds annually to enhance program initiatives.

Applied a wide range of qualitative and quantitative analytic and evaluative methods and techniques to assess and improve the Compliance program's effectiveness and reach.

Written Communication: communicated in writing with diverse internal and external audiences about research and evaluation (including research needs and priorities, building and using evidence, research methods, and research findings and implications). Consistently independently prepared written products that required little or no revision.

Oral Communication: communicated verbally through presentations, briefings, and conversations with diverse internal and external audiences about research and evaluation (including research needs and priorities, building and using evidence, research methods, and research findings and implications).

Executive Administrative Assistant   03/2012 – 02/2014
Allstate, Chicago, IL   40 hours/week
Supervisor: Richard Allen, 555-523-5321 (May Contact)   Annual Salary: $70,000

Supported department with routine daily administrative tasks. Provided comprehensive and diversified administrative support by applying in-depth knowledge of department policy, organization, and communication. Processed and prepared presentations and documents and solved problems related to specific tasks.

- ***Managed complex screening, fielding, and prioritization*** *of inbound communications through telephone, mail, and email. Achieved a 30% reduction in response times for critical issues, ensuring timely resolution and mitigating potential disruptions. The improvement enhanced overall organizational responsiveness and client satisfaction.*

Evaluated and managed financial and disbursing systems, resulting in a 20% reduction in system-related errors and a 15% increase in transaction processing efficiency. These improvements optimized financial operations and reduced operational costs.

Analyzed and applied functions, goals, objectives, work processes, and funding sources into anticipated or actual dollar figures, resulting in a 25% improvement in financial reporting accuracy over the next 12 months.

Improved the preparation and scheduling of activities, resulting in an increase in meeting and event efficiency. This time-saving enhancement allowed for more strategic use of personnel hours and contributed to a reduction in administrative costs related to event planning and travel coordination, saving the organization $30,000 annually.

Monitored office expenses, ensuring adherence to budget guidelines. Achieved a 100% budget adherence rate through expense review and coordination. Streamlined the accounts payable process, reducing invoice processing time and enhancing operational efficiency.

Interacted effectively with a variety of coworkers, supervisors, and subordinates.
- **Presented information** on specific research and evaluation goals and needs with senior management and contract representatives.
- **Briefed senior management** on complex research and evaluation issues or similar topics.
- **Assisted with the preparation**, planning, and hosting of research and evaluation conferences or meetings.
- **Served on panels, committees, or task forces** relating to technical and/or programmatic research and evaluation issues.
- **Regularly consulted** by my supervisor on technical research and evaluation issues.
- **Briefed coworkers and employees** on research and evaluation issues.

Education

Summa Cum Laude **B.S., Business Management,** The University of Chicago, Chicago, IL, GPA 3.9, 05/2011.
- *Relevant Coursework, Licenses, and Certifications*: MG 260 Business Law; EC 315 Quantitative Research Methods; IDS 375 Business Statistics II; ACTG 484 International Accounting

Select Job-Related Training

Machine Learning for Finance
Udemy Financial Analysis and Modeling Bootcamp
Advanced Data Analytics, LinkedIn Learning
Management Development Course
Managerial Research Analysis Course
Financial Analysis and Valuation for Strategic Decision-making
Quantitative Research Methods Course

Professional References

Brad Smith, Project Manager, Bsmith32@doe.gov, 555-325-2324

Susan Sanders, Executive Officer, U.S. Army, SusanSanders@us.army.mil, 555-325-2324

Phillip Johnson, Manager, JPMorgan Chase, PJonny34@gmail.com, 555-625-2322

Emily Brook, Commander, U.S. Army, Ebrook23@us.army.mil, 555-425-2321

Additional Information

Technical Skills: Microsoft Office Suite; Oracle PeopleSoft, Microsoft Teams, Salesforce, SQL, Python, Hyperion Financial Management

Generally, you should be leading with relevant action verbs that you can find both in the OPM job series handbook and within the job announcement in the "specialized experience" and "duties" sections. Lead with those verbs, and then write out your achievement using details. When you think you are done with your resume, review it a couple of more times and not just as a person who has accomplished the achievements. Look at your resume from the perspective of someone who doesn't know you, and then look at your resume from the perspective of someone who is actively trying to disqualify your resume. Identify the weaknesses. If you were HR, how would you disqualify your resume? Most of the time, we read our resumes with the benefit of having done the work and not as an outsider. After your reviews, you need to have another person read the resume with the intention of spotting errors or weaknesses. This is not the time to be prideful. Be willing to take the criticism and make the necessary adjustments. This is the only way to develop a competitive resume that will stand out from the competition.

In USAJob.gov, you are allowed to upload or create up to five resumes. Make sure you have an uploaded resume for each job series that you are targeting. You can also select to have one of your resumes searchable. This will allow the government to search for your resume based on the experience they are looking for. People have actually been contacted for an interview without applying to a job announcement solely based on having their resume searchable, so select the resume that aligns with the job series in which you most want to work.

Take action:

First, build your federal resume around a specific job series and then adjust it to the job announcement before applying on USAJobs.gov.

YOU ARE REFERRED

When you start applying for jobs on USAJobs.gov, you will eventually start getting referral notifications in your email. Should you celebrate it? I wouldn't. Don't get me wrong, it is a positive indicator, but so many referrals never turn into interviews. There is no obligation to interview you based on a referral.

A referral is when Human Resources (HR) determines you are the best-qualified applicant and passes your information over to the hiring manager. The hiring manager can then decide to interview you and hire you, but you must make it past HR before you even have a chance. HR will review your self-assessment questionnaire, your resume, and any other required documents, and then they'll make a list of the top-qualified applicants; these people are usually considered "best qualified." They'll send this list with all application materials to the hiring manager. The hiring manager will then go through this list and see if there's anybody that they'd like to interview. The hiring manager can decide to interview everyone or nobody.

Ideally, you want to see your job application turned into a referral, and then your referral turns into an invitation to interview. After you complete your interview(s), references are checked, and you receive a tentative job offer, undergo a background check, and then receive the final job offer. Here are some rough timelines that you can expect:

Referral 1–3 weeks after applying to the job announcement

<u>Interview</u> 2–6 weeks after getting the referral

<u>Tentative Job Offer</u> 3–4 weeks after interview

<u>Background check</u> 1 week–1 year, depending on the level of job risk

<u>Final Job Offer</u> 2–3 weeks after background check

Remember, these are very rough timelines, and with over four hundred different federal agencies, your time will largely depend upon the human resource office, the hiring manager, the security team, and the budget. Any delays with any one of those groups will result in a longer hiring process. The federal hiring process is a lot longer than the hiring process in the private sector. Overall, it should take four to six months on average to hire someone. I have seen this take three months and over a year in some situations. The time starts when you submit your job application on USAJobs.gov and stops when you begin your first day at work or EOD (Enter on Duty).

When you receive a notification email informing you that you were referred to a government job, you should smile and nod. It's a small signal that what you are doing is working. Your resume and the job announcements that you are targeting are a good fit, and you should continue to apply. There's a specific success formula I have developed that can determine whether your resume is strong enough and could predict when you will eventually get the job offer.

Take action:

When you get referred, smile and then keep applying.

SUCCESS FORMULA

I have noticed some similarities when helping and tracking over five hundred people who receive their federal government job offers. I have found that the main indicator of resume strength was at least a 50% referred rate. This means that if a person applies to a hundred job announcements on USAJob.gov, if they were referred at least fifty times, this would be a strong indicator of a good resume. From all referrals, I saw a roughly 20% interview request rate. This means that if a person had twenty referrals, then they should have received about four interview invitations. If this same person had prepared for the interview by having multiple mock interviews and rehearsing their success stories, then about 35–50% of those interviews would have resulted in job offers.

Let's go through that again:

- 50% referral rate
- 20% interview requests from referrals
- 35–50% job offer from interview

It is important to track the exact number of applications so that you can identify if your resume is the problem. Consider using a Microsoft Excel spreadsheet or Notion to create a job tracker that shows when you applied to the job, the position title, the federal agency, the GS grade, and the current status at a minimum. It can take a few weeks to start hearing whether you have been referred or not. Do not solely rely on the statuses within the USAJobs.gov website because it might not always be accurate. The responsibility of updating the statuses is on the federal agency, and they do not always do it in a timely manner.

If you are not getting anywhere near the numbers mentioned above, then it could be an indicator that you have a resume problem, the job announcements you are applying to are not aligned with your experience, or you need to spend more time tailoring your existing resume to the job announcement. This means you either need to improve your resume or stop applying to jobs that you are not eligible/qualified for. Now, this formula is not an exact science, but this is what I have witnessed with hundreds of applicants applying throughout the years on USAJobs.gov.

Take action:

Create a Microsoft Excel or Notion spreadsheet to track your referral and interview rate. If the referral rate falls before 50% or your interview rate falls below 20%, revisit your resume.

THE UNTOLD TRUTHS

I would love to sit here and tell you that nepotism doesn't exist anymore, and that it's made up, but then I would be lying. The practice of hiring friends and family is still alive and well in the federal government, but it isn't always easily detected. Take this experience for an example. I was working in Washington D.C. for one of the largest federal agencies in the government, and my boss told me that she was hiring a Program Analyst for our team, but despite interviewing six different candidates, she didn't think any of them would be a good fit for the position. She decided to ask Human Resources to repost the job announcement and interview some more people next month, but a couple of hours later, her colleague pulled her aside in the hallway and asked her if she had the chance to interview Jeremy yet because he was her son-in-law and she was interested in how he performed. My boss said she did interview him and that he did well, which was obviously not true because she just told the team she didn't select anyone. The next time she spoke with Human Resources, it wasn't to tell them to repost the job announcement; it was to confirm her selection of Jeremy, my new coworker. Luckily for me, Jeremy turned out to be a decent employee and a fine team member, but the way that he was hired raised a lot of eyebrows.

Nepotism is prohibited in the federal government, but it is still hardwired into a lot of humans, and it will probably never be completely eliminated from people or employment practices, so how can we benefit from it existing? You need to become known. You can become known in two different ways:

1. You are a current federal employee

    If you are already working as a federal employee, you need to volunteer and assist other people around you. You also need to be known for your usefulness and your work ethic. People will notice you, and you will start to build up your goodwill capital, and when a position opens up in your office or the adjacent office, you could be in a good position for the job.

2. You are not a federal employee

    If you are not a federal employee, you should be attending hiring events both virtual and in person. You are doing this to meet and potentially develop relationships with Human Resource Specialists, Job Coordinators, and Hiring Managers at different federal agencies. You are communicating your value and desire to work in their agencies. Attending these events will also give you information about the different job opportunities in these agencies.

    You should also be talking to people who are already working for the federal government. This is typically called an "informational interview," and it is a part of networking. Informational interviews and networking are a value exchange with another person. The value they're giving you is information about the federal agency, federal resumes, or the hiring process, and you are giving value by offering them a coffee or tea or other information that could be useful to them.

Hiring managers are not required to interview everyone who was referred to them, even if the applicants are the best qualified. If a hiring manager interviews six or 16 people, they are still not required to select anyone. Also, hiring managers are typically busy with managing their offices, attending meetings, and dealing with their other responsibilities, so scheduling interviews can sometimes end up at the bottom of their priority list, and that is why it can take a while to get an interview invitation.

Most of the time, you being qualified is not enough to get an interview or to get a job offer. This is why you are spending the extra time strengthening the achievements in your resume and you are spending the additional time preparing for the interview. Never think that just because you are qualified for the job, you should automatically receive it. Too many people lose sight of the fact that the hiring process is a competition, and just like any other competition, you have to find your edge and have a strong performance. Think about the hundreds of other people who are competing against you and find ways that you can send a clear signal that you are more qualified than them. It's not just you who wants a specific government job; oftentimes, it is dozens or hundreds of people who want it just as bad.

There are situations where the hiring manager knows exactly who they want to hire, but they still have to post a public job announcement on USAJobs.gov. This is because, by law, competitive service government jobs have to be posted publicly. Here is a scenario that has happened in the past: A lady is working a GS-12 government job and decides to take a "detail" opportunity, which means she is volunteering to work in another office outside of her current position. The details last six months, and then she returns to her office. A few weeks later, the same position she had just volunteered for was posted on USAJobs.gov as a GS-13 position, and the intention was for the lady who was on the "detail" to apply and get the job, which would result in a promotion. But even though she applied, she didn't make it past HR, so even though other people were referred, the job announcement was canceled, and she was told to strengthen her resume. Then, next week, the same job announcement was reposted with the intention of having her apply for the job again and hopefully get referred by HR.

When you become a federal employee, understand that "detail" opportunities are sometimes used as a trial to see if you will be a good fit for the position before the hiring manager has the job announcement posted. Too many federal employees ignore going into detail because they view it as extra work with no reward.

Unfortunately, poor performers are selected during the interview, and in other situations, the hiring manager decides not to do an interview. Government jobs that hire without interviews are usually below the GS-11 level. But it can be incredibly frustrating when a person is selected over you for a promotion or job, and you know for a fact that they are not as qualified as you. Instead of being upset or resentful, you should refocus your eyes on your own journey, keep doing the actions that drive progress, and you will get your job offer. There are many people with no special hiring paths and who know absolutely nobody on the inside, and they're getting government job offers every day. The main reason that people are not successful in getting a federal government job is not because they're not eligible, not qualified, or failed an interview. The main reason people don't get the job offer is because they quit. That's the only way you will not succeed if you quit.

There are thousands of people around the country who believe you cannot get into the federal government at a high level with high pay. I'm talking about jobs in the GS-14 or GS-15 level, which have salaries of $150k and above. They have the misconception that you must start at the bottom of the ladder, such as GS-5 to GS-7, and then slowly climb your way up, and after many years, you finally reach the top. That idea is false. The only two things that determine your GS grade level are your experience and location. If you have the required experience and are willing to travel anywhere, then you could come into the federal government as a GS-15 or even higher, such as a Senior Executive or a Senior Leader. I have witnessed people leave the military one week and enter the federal government as a GS-15 the next week. The main reason you will continue to hear people talk about "just get your foot in the door" by taking a lower GS grade level is because that is what they were told, and it's what they did, so now they think you must do the same. Do not believe it. It will result in you losing tens of thousands of dollars in your first month of employment. If you have the relevant experience, do not sell yourself short. You have to be your biggest advocate.

Take action:

Understand that the hiring process can be unfair, and make a commitment to never quit

INTERVIEW OBSTACLES

It's exciting when you start getting invitations to interview. Usually, this comes to you in an email, but occasionally, it could be a phone call. The email will have multiple time slots for you to select from, and it will give you an idea of how many other people will be interviewed. Some people choose the first time slot so they can impress the hiring panel/hiring manager immediately, and others select the last time slot so that they can leave a strong, lasting impression. Pick any time slot you would like, as I don't think it matters that much.

Interviews are usually in a structured panel format, but they could also be one-on-one with the hiring manager. If your interview is a panel, then you should understand a few things:

1. You're being scored during the interview on a scoresheet
2. Your answers are probably being written down or recorded
3. It will feel like a cold & distant environment
4. All the questions are the same for all candidates

Since 2020, a lot more interviews have been done virtually through Microsoft Teams or Zoom. Other interviews will be a simple phone call with multiple people on the line.

Regardless of the format, you will notice that the interview will feel lifeless, awkward, or distant. People on the panel will usually not make small talk, laugh at your jokes, or rephrase their questions, and you might take this personally or use it as an indicator that you are not performing well. But it doesn't have anything to do with you or your performance; this is the way the majority of federal government interviews are conducted.

It still surprises me just how many people willingly admit to me that they did not prepare for their job interviews. Interviews can sometimes be hard to come by, so if you get invited to an interview, you need to block off time in your life to properly prepare; otherwise, do not be surprised when you are not selected for the job.

Now, let's discuss the best way you can prepare for a federal government interview. The first step is to take another look at the job announcement that you are interviewing for. If you don't remember where the job announcement is, I would ask the HR Specialist (the person setting up the interview) for a copy of the job announcement. This is important because you will find three areas in the job announcement that will greatly increase your odds of getting the job offer.

In all three of these areas, you are writing success stories. These should be accomplishments that are similar to the success stories in your resume. Create at least a total of 10 success stories in the STAR (Situation, Task, Action, Result) or CAR (Context, Action, Result) format for these sections of the job announcement:

1. Specialized Experience

   You will find verbs in this paragraph that are required for the job you are applying to. If it mentions that the experience required is a person who has drafted, reviewed, and edited documents, then you need to have a success story that speaks directly to those verbs.

2. Duties

   This section plainly explains what a person will be doing on the job. You want to be that person, so use the words in this section to create a success story of how you have already done those tasks and how you have done them at a high level.

3. Questionnaire

   You can preview the questionnaire in some job announcements. Otherwise, you will have to look in your job application on USAJobs.gov to find it. The reason you are looking in here is that sometimes the Questionnaire has different verbs than the "Specialized Experience" or "Duties" section, so it is worth reviewing again to pick up any other requirements you think the job might have and create a success story that speaks to it.

So, how would a strong Success Story look? Here's an example of a STAR Success Story that is focused on the 0343 job series, highlighting the verbs "analyze" and "evaluate":

(Situation) I was working as Senior Military Science Instructor at Elizabeth City State University in Elizabeth City, NC. My cadets were struggling with their tactical evaluations (receiving failing scores) in the training exercises and poor performance at the end-of-the-year capstone stone evaluation at Fort Knox, KY. As a result, some had to repeat the year, which delayed their commissioning date, or suffered from low scores, which negatively impacted their branch of choice. Also, it negatively impacted the reputation of the Military Science program at the university.

(Task) Increase the cadets' end-of-year scores

(Action) I analyzed and evaluated the students' knowledge gap by studying capstone spreadsheets. I then completely reconstructed the following year's military science curriculum by adding valuable lessons and removing irrelevant topics, creating new dynamic PowerPoint slides with video, sound, and animation, developing customized quizzes, and creating new relevant practical exercises to better prepare the next class for the annual capstone event.

(Results) Our ROTC program capstone event rose from a 70% pass rate to a 90% pass rate over the following 12 months. My unit met its commissioning goal, which is set by the Army, for the fiscal year. I also earned a strong performance evaluation and was directly commended by my senior supervisor.

That is one example, but I want you to have at least ten success stories, and you need to write them down. If there are only five verbs listed on the job announcement, create two success stories for each verb. You are getting these verbs from two areas of the job announcement: 1. the Specialized Experience section and 2. the Duties section. When writing a success story, try to include two or three key verbs in each story; that way, you will be able to pivot and give the same success story to different types of questions the interviewer may be asking you. You should write down your success stories, read them, and rehearse them multiple times in a mock interview so that they become a part of your memory, and during the actual interview, you will be able to communicate your success story in a confident and conversational tone.

If you are having a hard time creating a success story, you need to look at your past performance reviews, awards, and certificates and remind yourself of what your accomplishments were. Remember that even though your actions may have seemed small, they can still have large impacts on an organization. If your company proudly stated that it grew revenue by 20% quarter over quarter, look for how your actions might have contributed to that result. If your previous office passed a compliance inspection by 100%, then your actions contributed to that result. A lot of times, we downplay our experience, and we can easily forget what we have accomplished.

You might be wondering, what happens if they ask me a question that I wasn't expecting and I can't use one of my success stories? The way we are preparing our success stories is for them to have multiple uses. If the interviewer asks about communication skills, analytical skills, database skills, or collaboration skills, we can still give them the same sample success story from above. We just need to highlight different verbs. So, when someone asks you a random question during the interview, find a way to make one of your success stories fit it.

The next step in interview preparation is for you to research the federal agency's mission and/or vision statement. You will find what is important to the agency in this statement. Try to speak to the agency's mission during your introduction, or if they ask you the question, "Why do you want to work for this agency?" I would also do a quick Google search to see if there are any current events happening within the agency. This can clearly set you apart from other people who didn't take a few minutes to research the agency.

As your interview is coming to an end, oftentimes, you will be asked if you have any questions for the panel or for the hiring manager. The answer is always yes. Asking questions shows that you are curious and that you have a genuine interest in accepting the job. If you do not ask any questions, it usually shows that you do not care. But do not just ask any random question; make sure that your questions are thoughtful. Some examples of this would be:

- Why do you like working here?
- What are some of the pain points your office is experiencing?
- What would this position be focused on for the first 3 to 6 months of hire?
- When do you plan on making a selection for this position?
- Can you describe the culture in your office?

In some rare cases, you may be given the exact interview questions 15–30 minutes before the interview, and if they do this with you, then you can be sure that they are doing this with all the candidates. This can be a document with eight to ten questions, and you can use this time to quickly write down some notes and think about the exact way you plan to answer those questions.

After your interview, it can usually take between one to three weeks to hear anything back. If it has been over three weeks and you still haven't heard anything, email the HR Specialist or person who scheduled the initial interview and politely ask for a status update. Continue to do this on a three-week interval until they tell you the result.

Some federal agencies will want to do a second interview with the top two or three candidates. The secondinterview is usually a lot less formal, and it will probably be a one-on-one chat with the hiring manager to make sure you are a good fit. The only situation I have seen it go beyond two interviews is in the following example:

- 1st interview with team members (your future co-workers)
- 2nd interview with hiring manager (your future boss)
- 3rd interview is really just a meet and greet with the executive

After interviewing, many times HR will reach out to you asking if it's okay to contact your references. This is a good indicator that you are being seriously considered for the position. A lot of federal agencies will not spend the time calling your references unless you are one of the top candidates. However, other agencies, such as the Department of Defense, have been known to call your references even before the interview starts to save time, so this will be agency-dependent, but having your references contacted is a good sign.

During the interview, if you feel that you are doing poorly or if your mind blanks, keep going. There have been so many times where a person feels they did absolutely horrible in the interview, and a couple of weeks later, they are surprised to see a job offer in their inbox. If you struggle to give an answer, give them one of your success stories, even if it does not seem relevant to the question being asked. Any answer is usually better than no answer. This is especially true during the structured interviews that are being scored. It is better to get one point for a poor answer than zero points for not even trying to give an answer. Finish the interview strong, and remember that you are never out of consideration.

While you are waiting for the result of the interview or the job offer, do not sit idle. You need to keep applying to other job announcements. Regardless of how amazing you think the interview went, there is no guarantee that you will get the job. This is true even when you have a job offer because job offers can be rescinded for many reasons. Above all else, keep applying as you are waiting on the interview results.

Take action:

Prepare for your interview by writing at least ten success stories that speak to the words in the job announcement.

THE JOB OFFER

The first job offer you receive will likely be a tentative job offer (TJO), and it will come to your email inbox. This email will often have a link that will take you to a USAHire website so you can formally click a button to accept, decline, or select that you wish to speak with HR. I recommend that you accept the job offer; you can always talk to HR later, and you can always reject the job offer in the future. Immediately after accepting the TJO, I would start to negotiate your salary, but we will talk more about that later.

After you accept it, you will probably receive more emails with onboarding documents, and sometimes, you will be required to upload these documents into the USAHire system; other times, it will be done through email. Once the documents have been submitted, you are going to be waiting for the security team to start your background check. At a minimum, this usually requires fingerprints, pictures, credit checks, and criminal background checks. This can vary depending on the federal agency and the position you will be in. Government jobs that are classified as high-risk or jobs that require a secret or top-secret clearance can further extend the hiring process.

When you are connected with the security team, remember that they move at their own pace depending on their workload, and if you want to check in on the hiring process, you still need to communicate with the Human Resource Specialist who extended you the job offer. Many people try to bypass the HR Specialist and directly ask the security team point of contact about an updated status, but that is usually not the person you should be talking to.

After your background is checked, Human Resources should send you the final job offer (FJO). It is important to check every piece of information on the offer. Your information should be accurate, and it should also mention if the job is in competitive service, excepted service, or senior executive service, if there are any relocation expenses authorized or incentive bonuses, and it should also have your start date on the offer. If any information is missing or inaccurate, you need to communicate it to HR.

The start date, or what the government calls EOD (entrance on duty), is your first day at work. This is usually when you take an oath of office and your orientation begins. You will learn all about the federal agency you will be working in through various speakers and PowerPoint slides. Many times, HR will ask you to pick a start date before the final job offer is sent, so the date on the job offer should have been agreed upon, and it should not come as a surprise.

Once you sign to accept the job offer, you should celebrate but understand that the job is not completely secure until you are sitting in the chair on the first day of work. Unfortunately, federal agencies can still rescind or cancel your job offer, even if it is a final job offer. I have spoken to people who have already packed up the moving truck and rented their house to travel across the country just to be told that their job offer was rescinded. Job offers can get rescinded for a lot of different reasons, including budget issues, restructuring, or a change in mission. You might not even get a reason why the job offer is being rescinded.

The good news is that this is rare. If the federal agency has already spent the time and resources necessary to do a background check and to dedicate an HR Specialist to the hiring process, when you do receive a final job offer, I believe you have a 95% chance of it being secure. But this is another reason why I'm encouraging you to keep applying to job announcements until you are sitting in your new chair in your new office, regardless of how many interviews or job offers you have.

You also reserve the right to reject a job offer at any stage of the hiring process. You are never "locked in." This isn't the military, and there is no mandatory contract that forces you to stay at the job. You might feel guilty for rejecting a job offer, especially if you have already accepted a tentative job offer, and now it feels like you are backing out from the agency that was trying to give you an opportunity. But there is no naughty list that your name is put on that will shut you out of future government employment opportunities, even if you do reject job offers. Everyone supporting the hiring process understands that the candidate has to do what is in their best interest, and nobody should be angry or resentful.

Take action:

Accept all tentative job offers and review them for accuracy.

THE NEGOTIATIONS

Many people have no idea that they can negotiate a federal government job offer, but it's possible, and people are doing it every day. If you are new to the federal government, you are allowed to negotiate three areas, this includes:

1. Salary (Step level)
2. Leave Accrual Rate
3. Start Date

But most people will completely skip the negotiation step, and if you make the decision to skip, you could be leaving tens of thousands of dollars on the table. Over the span of three to four years, it could easily exceed the cost of $100,000 that you could have had. So, why in the world would people skip this step? The main reason people skip this step is because:

1. Nobody prompts them to negotiate
2. They do not want to extend the hiring process
3. They feel they are putting the job offer at risk
4. They do not know how

You have to be the one that initiates the negotiation, and it is true that by negotiating, you will be adding time to the overall hiring process, but for many of us, it is more than worth it. Immediately after accepting the tentative job offer, you should email the HR Specialist a memo that clearly explains why you are a "Superiorly Qualified Candidate." In the past, federal agencies were able to use your past earning statement or pay stub to justify an increase in step level (increase in salary), but that was recently determined to be discriminatory, so that practice will no longer take place. Instead, you will be communicating your experience, specifically highlighting the following areas if they apply to you:

- You have many years of experience doing relevant work
- You have many certifications in your field
- You have special or hard-to-find certificates that are relevant
- You taught the subject in class
- You have published work in peer-reviewed journals
- You have a relevant graduate degree

Human Resources will then determine whether you are a "Superiorly Qualified Candidate" or not. If you are eligible, the decision still lies with the federal agency. The agency could refuse to negotiate with you based on an existing policy letter or for any other reason. Most federal agencies will negotiate with you if you have the right experience, but in some situations, such as job announcements using the "Recent Students Graduate" or "Students" pathway, then it is highly unlikely you will be able to negotiate your step level.

If you want or need a higher salary, then you are trying to negotiate a higher step level. Regardless of your experience and education and regardless of the GS grade, you will probably be offered Step 1 in your tentative job offer. The problem with taking Step 1 is that it usually takes 18 years to move from Step 1 to Step 10, which is the maximum step level in the GS pay band. I have seen multiple people successfully negotiate up to Step 10 based on their experience. I have also seen highly qualified people accept Step 1. Today, the difference between Step 1 and Step 10 can be up to $28,000 a year. If you are wondering what Step level you should ask for, ask yourself the following questions:

- What salary is reasonable for someone in the private market with your skills and experience?
- What salary do you need?
- What salary are you currently making?

When you negotiate, sometimes the federal agency will counteroffer, and an example of this is if you request a GS-12, step 7, and the agency then offers you a GS-12, step 4. Should you accept it? I would accept it. If you decide to negotiate further, it could result in your job offer being rescinded, and they can move on to another candidate. The only time I would continue to negotiate is if you are fully prepared to step away from the job offer. This is another reason it is important to try to get multiple job offers.

When negotiating your step level, it can add additional time to the entire hiring process. This could add weeks to your starting the job, and one of the frustrating parts of this waiting is that the communication between you and the federal agency isn't always the best. You have to ask yourself if it is worth it to you based on your situation.

No matter how qualified you are, the federal agency gets the last word in step negotiations, and they could decide not to do it for any reason, but it's still worth trying. Once you are a current federal employee, you are no longer allowed to negotiate step levels when accepting other government job offers unless there is a 90-day or more break in service.

As a federal employee, if you are considering taking a lower GS grade job in the future, there is a function called "pay-setting" federal agencies can choose to do in order to minimize the overall loss in your salary. For example, if you are working in a GS-12, step 3 job and decide to accept a GS-11 job offer in another state, the agency can try to increase the step level of your GS-11 job to try to match the salary of a GS-12, step 3. Once again, this is optional, and it remains at the agency's discretion.

Take action:

Create a memo explaining why you are a Superiorly Qualified Candidate and have it ready to send as soon as you accept your tentative job offer.

WHAT TO EXPECT

You will be a little nervous on your first day of work, but that is completely normal. You don't know what you're doing. None of us did. It takes a while to understand the agency, the different processes, people's names, and the additional projects we could be working on. Most government supervisors and leaders understand that you are in the learning phase and you are not going to be able to "hit the ground running." Do not let the pressure of learning something new keep you from sleeping at night or worrying if you will be terminated because of your performance.

Almost all federal employees are initially on a 12-month probationary period, and in other situations, it could be twenty-four months. During this time, you can be terminated for any reason, just like a private sector "at-will" employee. However, the majority of federal employees make it through this period with no problems. I think, on average, over 95% of new federal employees survive and get past the probationary period. However, some people make the wrong decisions, and it costs them their jobs. Here are some common reasons for termination:

- Chronic lateness
- Failure to show up
- Falsifying your timecard
- Theft or Assault

If you show up with the desire to learn, a good attitude, and a willingness to help, you will greatly reduce the chances of being terminated in the probationary period. After probation, you are granted additional protections and will have appeal rights for any termination actions. If you are in a competitive service government job, then after three years, you will be a "status candidate." This means that you can leave the government to the private sector or just take a break, and then when you apply back to the government, you are still eligible for the competitive service hiring path, which greatly expands the job opportunities you are eligible for.

I also think you shouldn't be still for too long. It's great that you were able to get your first federal government job, but for many jobs, you need to apply to another job announcement to get promoted. The exception is if you are in a job that has a built-in promotion ladder. Many government jobs do not have this. So, you could accept a GS-6 or GS-7 and just stay there for decades if you do not decide to search and apply for other job announcements.

If you find yourself in a toxic work environment, immediately start applying for a position on USAJobs.gov again. I have talked to many people who quickly discovered their supervisor did not like them, or their supervisor seemed to be looking for reasons to terminate them because of a personality conflict. In other situations, the office could have a much faster work tempo than you are accustomed to, and you might be looking for a different type of work environment. I helped a lady leave a job at the Department of Agriculture after just three months on the job because she could not stand how her supervisor was talking to her during meetings. You can leave for any reason at any time, but you will not have any options unless you frequently apply for other jobs.

As a current federal employee, one advantage you have is the internal hiring path, which federal agencies can use to hire people inside of their agency. Many hiring managers believe it's a benefit to hire a known person; they already know their work ethic, their accomplishments, and their reputation in the office. How much this path will benefit you will depend on the size of the federal agency. There are more internal hire positions in the Department of Defense simply because it's the largest agency in the federal government. Instead, if you worked for the Selective Service System, you might not have any internal hire opportunities because that agency only has a little over a hundred employees.

Most federal employees are allowed two 15-minute breaks and 30 minutes for lunch every day. Some supervisors will allow their employees to combine that time into one hour, but you should ask. Every federal agency office has its own unique culture. How much you enjoy working in your office will depend largely on your direct supervisor and the executive responsible for your section. Some offices are typically more high-paced and high-stress than others, such as the OCFO (Office of the Chief Financial Officer). You will largely have no idea what to expect until you start working in the office. There are a few actions I believe you can take to best prepare you for your new job, consider:

- Learn the office acronyms
- Learn the hierarchy

- Read the SOP (Standard of Procedures)
- Offer to assist coworkers to learn more

Most people understand it will take at least one to two years to fully understand your role and to be proficient in your job, and even then, there will be plenty that you do not know. Try to identify who the subject matter expert is on different systems and processes as soon as you start working so you know who you can rely on to get the necessary information. When you frequently offer to assist your coworkers and people in other offices, you are building up "goodwill" capital that you can leverage when you need the most help. It can take a long time to complete basic tasks when it involves many other people, especially when they are not required to help you.

Take action:

Create a list of actions you need to focus on during your first week of work. Do not be afraid to ask questions; people expect you to.

WORKING TO DEATH

If you are reading this and have a job in the private sector, what is it offering you? The only reason you should stay in a job is if it is making your life better. That is the agreement: you bring value to an organization, and that organization makes your life better. Is your current job making your life better? Or will they terminate you tomorrow without a second thought? Are you earning a secure retirement, and are you being challenged and developed? So many people settle for an average job when they are capable of so much more. If you do not make the effort to find something better by searching or talking to new people then there will be thousands of better opportunities you will never find out about.

You must care about your future more than anyone. Your family and friends might want the best for you, but you are your best advocate for a better future. You can easily put all of your energy and time toward a job that will not contribute one single penny to your retirement. When you enter your mid-sixties, seventies, and eighties, what will allow you to live your life in dignity? Are you going to be completely dependent on your family? Federal government jobs still offer pensions, and with the volatility of the stock market, pensions are still the most stable and secure source of income that you can count on when you decide to retire. The federal pension is separate from your social security check, and it is not connected to the stock market. Many federal employees choose to use their Thrift Savings Plan at retirement and do not even have the need to touch the money from their pension so that money can continue to build in their savings account.

I walk into restaurants, gas stations, and retail stores around Virginia on a daily basis and ask people who are making $12 to $15 an hour, what is the plan? What will your next job be? Have you been applying? What I usually get in return is a blank stare of confusion. This could be because I'm a complete stranger or because they haven't thought about their future. They do not know what is next; there is no aim toward a goal, and they are simply floating through life without much thought of their future. People need an aim, even if it is not a federal government job, to strive for a better position. The problem is that a higher-paying job will usually not fall into your lap without you making the effort, getting uncomfortable, and taking action toward it. The actions are:

1. Align your skills with a better job
2. Identify any skill gaps and close them
3. Improve your resume
4. Talk to people who are where you want to be
5. Apply and keep applying!

Do you have a three-year or five-year plan? If not, create one. What you do today will have a huge impact on how life looks for you in the near future. Are you volunteering, reading, improving your skills, and building relationships?

If you are earning 50k a year this year, in three years, that number shouldn't be the same. Identify a goal that you want to achieve; maybe it's 65k in salary or more. It doesn't have to involve your salary. Maybe you want a higher-level position so that you can impact more people or more areas. What would it take for you to get there?

Do not allow yourself to stop growing because you feel safe or comfortable in your current job. Continue to challenge yourself with new experiences. Life becomes incredibly boring, and it's easy to feel resentment when you do not at least try for more in all aspects of your life. People tend to reject themselves from a job before they even apply. Despite your doubts, at least try. Let other people be the ones that tell you "no." And when the "no's" start to come, do not take a step back; instead, step into the rejections and find areas that you can improve and keep striving for more. It is not greedy or wrong to want more from life. It is human, and when you are paid more and have more resources, you will be able to benefit the people around you that you care for a lot more.

LANDS OF DESPAIR

When you are deep in the job searching phase, it's normal to become deeply discouraged and even depressed. You've applied dozens of times. Why is nobody getting back to you? You start to question your value and your worth. These feelings become even worse if there are external pressures in your life. Maybe you are in a paycheck-to-paycheck situation, someone is depending upon you, or there is debt accumulating, and you are feeling helpless. This is what I like to call the lands of despair, but you can get through it. What will separate you from other job applicants is if and when you decide to quit applying. The main difference between a person who successfully receives their final job offer and a person who does not is how consistent and persistent that person is applying on USAJobs.gov. Have you committed to applying daily? How many times are you applying a day? How many job series are you targeting? Who has looked at your resume?

What will usually happen is a person will casually apply five to 10 times and then decide to stop due to frustration. Remember that when your job application is getting referred around 50% of the time, that is a positive indicator! When you start getting interview invitations, that is another positive indicator, and it means that your federal resume is working. If you are not getting referrals or interview requests, that simply means that you have to refocus on your federal resume and the job announcements you are applying to. You can have a strong resume, but it might not be relevant to the job announcements you are applying for. Taking a small amount of time to adjust your resume to the job announcement can pay off in a big way. Look at the verbs in the "specialized experience" section and search for those words in your resume. How many times are those words coming up? You should be creating success stories based on those verbs. If they are missing, add them to your achievements.

Before going to sleep, tell yourself that when you wake up, you will apply to at least three jobs before breakfast or at whatever time works best for you. You need to make a commitment to yourself and take action. It could be helpful to write it down on a piece of paper or set a reminder on your smartphone, but make sure you do it. You need to believe in yourself; if you lie to yourself, the whole system will come crashing down. So if you say it to yourself, make sure to do it. Once you apply, try to detach emotionally from that job announcement. Do not spend time thinking about it after you submit it. That would be time wasted. Instead, focus on the next job announcement and keep applying. It is easy to start daydreaming about the perfect job and wonder if you will ever get the referral or interview. Doing that is a time trap; you are losing time that could be spent on the actions that are necessary to reach your goal more quickly.

Surprisingly, a large chunk of resumes that people use when applying to federal government jobs are not strong, and many times, the resumes are not even decent. Many people mass apply to jobs they are not qualified for with one-page private sector resumes. This is called the "spray and pray" method, and it is not effective. So, you are actually competing with 50% of applicants who are at a decent level and above. Some job announcements only get a dozen applicants; you will be the applicant who stands out because of your relevant resume and the way you have prepared before the interview. I know the pain and sadness of this phase, and I also know that you are capable of getting through it. Stay committed to your plan and the actions, and you will make it out of the lands of despair.

Take action:

Create a list of actions you will do daily to move you toward a better job and a better future. Commit to doing the actions.

SUCCESS STORIES

I think it is helpful to include some success stories to show you exactly how other people were able to get their federal government jobs. I hope these stories can inform and inspire you to take action in your own journey toward a better job.

RECONNECTING WITH A FRIEND | GS-9

I randomly bumped into an old friend a few miles from a well-known Virginia university. I hadn't seen him in about a decade. I asked how he was doing, and he eventually told me that he was working as an administrative assistant at the local university. I asked him how much the job paid, and he told me it was around $45,000 a year. That didn't sound right to me. He had over fifteen years of work experience, and I was sure that he was settling for a below-average salary. He told me the job wasn't very challenging, and he would love to find a better job, but the job search was rough. He applied dozens of times on Indeed.com and wasn't having any luck. I asked him what type of jobs he was applying for, and he told me anything involving administrative work. But he wasn't sure what he was qualified for, and he jumped at the first job that would hire him. I told him that we were going to change that.

The following weekend, I met him at a cafe, and I explained the federal hiring process in detail over a cup of coffee. I showed him a federal resume template and said that if he transferred the information from his private resume to the federal resume template, I would do all the edits for him. I emphasized that the hiring process takes time, and it would be between four to six months before any job offers would arrive. He followed through and emailed me his resume a few days later. I quickly made multiple edits, which mainly included reorganizing his achievements by order of strength, elaborating on some of the details in his achievements, and adding skills I knew that he had but had overlooked. I then told him to start applying to the 0301 job series in volume with this exact resume. He assured me he would and thanked me for the help.

But would he? A lot of people tell you they will do things all the time, but rarely will they actually follow through with the advice and come back to let you know the result. I didn't think about his situation anymore; it wasn't until five or six weeks later that he called me one evening out of the blue and told me he had an interview with the Department of Defense for a GS-9 job. We prepared for the interview by creating his success stories related to the job announcement, and shortly after the interview, he received the job offer, and immediately, his salary jumped up by at least $20,000 a year. I congratulated him but stressed to him that he shouldn't get too comfortable there, and there was still a lot of room on the pay scale to climb.

Then, eighteen months later, he was motivated to apply for a GS-11 position in a different federal agency that was 100% remote, and he would eventually get the job offer for that job, too. He is now in a position that is completely different than when we first talked in the cafe. At that time, He was still living in his family's house and had a girlfriend. He wanted to take his relationship with his girlfriend to the next level, but he didn't have the resources to make it happen. Today, he has those resources. His life completely changed course in less than three years, and it's because he decided to give federal government jobs a try. He was serious about implementing the advice and didn't look back. At first, he had a little self-doubt, which is normal. He didn't think he would be eligible for a better-paying job, but like most people, he didn't know what he didn't know. I believe there are thousands of people just like my friend who are capable of earning tens of thousands of dollars more a year in salary, but they just do not know the opportunity exists.

FAMILY DOLLAR LADY | GS-12

A lady emailed me one evening and told me her story of successfully getting a job at Veterans Affairs using the information I provided her. She worked in retail all of her life, and she slowly progressed from working at Bed, Bath, & Beyond to the local Family Dollar store, and eventually, she reached the management level. The problem with that was she was working 70-hour weeks dealing with a lot of stressful store issues, and on top of that, the pay wasn't that great.

Like many people, she started working a retail job as a part-time job. It was never supposed to be a career, but she ended up staying and getting small pay raises, and one day, she realized that she had been working in retail for over 15 years. She didn't really know anything else, and she was afraid she would spend her entire life there. The problem with this: Besides the hours she was working, there was no pension. Most private sector jobs will not offer their employees a pension because it greatly cuts into business profits, and companies would rather have those profits go back to their shareholders and executives.

She had an old high school friend who had already been working a federal government job for 15 years, and she asked her friend for advice. Unfortunately, her friend wouldn't share her resume with her, but she did give some advice; she was told that she had to take a lower-salary job to "get her foot in the door," which was completely not true.

Her friend didn't mean any harm, but she just told her what she was told when she was looking for her first government job. The cycle of misinformation continues from one person to another. Thankfully, she didn't listen to her friend and started applying to a range of GS grades from GS-11 to GS-13. She made sure she had all the filters on USAJobs.gov saved and applied every day. At first, there weren't any results, and it was discouraging, but after about six weeks, she saw an email in her inbox for an invitation to interview. Her face lit up, and she experienced a flood of happiness. She quickly accepted the first job offer and decided not to negotiate her step level. I believe she should have tried to negotiate because that could have greatly increased her salary, but she was just happy to have the job.

Many people do not want to extend the already long hiring process or cause any disruptions by trying to negotiate the step level. Other people think that they could risk losing their job offer if they try to negotiate, but in the majority of cases, when people negotiate, they end up increasing their salary by thousands of dollars.

She intends to continue working for the federal government for at least the next ten years and might even try to change federal agencies in a few years. She is happy to report that her work-life balance is a lot better now. She doesn't have to worry about missing special occasions and holidays with her family. Also, she is now working toward a federal pension.

LEVERAGING A COORDINATOR | GS-11

Months before leaving the military, I went to a lot of federal hiring events, and this was before the pandemic, so they were all in-person events. One event I went to was hosted by the United States Patent and Trademark Office (USPTO) in Alexandria, VA. At the event, there was a Veteran Coordinator who was giving a presentation; she explained that she typically worked with other agency coordinators to assist veterans. Her main job was to help veterans with noncompetitive hiring authorities get hired into federal government jobs. At the time, I was not close enough to my military discharge date for her to consider working with me, but I still talked to her at length, and toward the end of the event, she gave me her business card.

The next week, I gave that same card to a friend of mine who was already out of the military. He was working at a university as a military science instructor and looking for a better job with benefits. His resume wasn't in the best shape, but he contacted her and sent her his resume. After a couple of weeks, she was able to arrange an interview with a hiring manager at the International Trade Administration for a GS-11 job. He went on the interview, performed well enough, and was offered the job right on the spot.

This friend never applied for a single job announcement on USAJobs.gov, and this government job was never advertised on USAJobs.gov. Many jobs under the excepted service do not need to be advertised on the website. If you are using a noncompetitive hiring authority, you can use a hiring coordinator to identify a lot of these different job opportunities. There are Schedule A and Veteran coordinators that you can email if you are eligible for those hiring paths. Your email should include your supporting documentation that proves you are eligible for the hiring authority and the job series you are targeting.

In his situation, the agency was able to use the VRA authority to put him in the government job. He was completely surprised the entire hiring process took about three months. He entered the government as a 0343 Management Analyst. He only planned to stay there for five years, and then he wanted to retire again. The first retirement was with the Army, and the second time will be from the federal government.

He is also receiving his military pension while working his federal government job. This is possible if you retire with at least twenty years of active-duty military service or if you are medically retired. If you have not retired from the military but still have active-duty time, you can buy back your time and add more years to increase your federal pension amount. In some cases, even people with 20-year military retirements still decide to buy back their time. If you are prior military, you should at least do the calculation to see if it will be worth it to you.

This story is one of the reasons I encourage people to take the time to attend federal hiring events; many of them are still virtual, so you do not have to get dressed and drive anywhere. Even if you are naturally introverted and do not like talking to strangers, make the effort to meet new people. You can attend the events from the comfort of your home, and you might get to meet a coordinator, a Human Resource Specialist, or a hiring manager. If you are a Veteran and would like a list of the latest Veteran coordinators by a federal agency, you can find their contact information on this website: https://www.opm.gov/fedshirevets/veteran-job-seekers/vets-agency-directory/

ARMY CAPTAIN TO DOD | GS-13

An Army Captain called me one evening and explained his background. He was an artillery officer who served in the military for six years, and he wanted to transition into the civilian world. Like most people transitioning from the military, he was experiencing some anxiousness and was uneasy about what was next for him in life. He wanted to keep his current lifestyle but didn't know if it was possible. He was willing to relocate, but he wanted to know what was a realistic GS grade range he could expect. I told him that if he was willing to come to the Washington D.C. area, he could realistically target GS-12 to GS-14. The next question was what government jobs I thought he would be eligible for with his combat background.

Many military members who work in combat fields do not think they have any transferable skills on the civilian side, and that is untrue. Even though combat soldiers spend a lot of their time in the field performing tactical drills, at the rifle range, or doing vehicle maintenance, there is still a lot of work that is done in the garrison. Every officer and noncommissioned officer in the military has some level of administrative experience. This experience comes from writing counseling, evaluations, and awards, preparing training documents, PowerPoint presentations, and operation orders, and conducting after-action reviews. Many people do not view this as administrative experience, but it is, and it is possible to go deep into the impact your actions had on the organization and build a competitive resume.

With his experience, he was clearly eligible for the 0301 Administration and Program, 0340 Program Manager, 0343 Management And Program Analysis, and 0346 Logistics Management job series. We focused on translating his combat experience into language that the Human Resource Specialist could understand and appropriately value. Most of the time, you do not need to mention words such as "combat," "warfighters," and "weapons" in your resume. It doesn't really add any value to the resume unless you are targeting a "weapons instructor" job announcement at the Department of Defense. The next step was to build his experience and responsibilities into compelling achievements that speak to both the job series and the job announcement.

Speaking of the Department of Defense (DoD), there are more federal agencies out there. One of the challenges of prior military members targeting DoD is that there is a 180-day rule which states that retired military members have to wait a period of 180 days immediately after retirement to be appointed to a DoD civilian position. There are waivers for this requirement, but it presents another barrier to the hiring process. So many people in the military hyperfocus on defense contracting or work for the Department of Defense of the Veterans Affairs because they think those are the only agencies that will value their experience, and that's not true. There are over four hundred federal agencies you could potentially work in, and if you do not want to work in an environment with a military culture, I would encourage you to explore other agencies.

He explained to me that his military transition class was unorganized and rushed, and he didn't think he was fully prepared to start applying for federal government jobs. I realigned him with what he was capable of and told him the importance of applying in volume and not getting discouraged. His entire journey from Army officer to federal government employee took him around four months, and after about 40 to 50 job applications and three interviews, he finally received his job offer email and was excited to start his first day of work out of uniform. On our last call, he confessed that he still missed the comradery of being in the military and being a commissioned officer in the Army, but his work-life balance dramatically improved, and he was excited about the future.

MY STORY

I think it is appropriate to end the Chapter with my own story. I joined the Army at the age of 17 with a GED (General Educational Development) certification. I stepped into an Army recruiter's office on a rainy day in Slidell, Louisiana. I decided to be a combat engineer, and I worked with demolitions largely in an outside environment for most of my career. Two things initially attracted me to the Army; the first was the idea of adventure, and the second was the ability to earn a pension after twenty years of military service. I went on many deployments and have been stationed at military bases all over the country, but as my career was closing in on the 20-year mark, I started to wonder what was next for my life. I didn't know how any of my military experience would fit with a traditional job. Should I try to get into law enforcement or maybe into sales? I started looking for federal government jobs about a year before leaving the Army. I searched all over the internet, from the government job Facebook groups, Reddit forums, OPM.gov and YouTube for any information that I thought would give me the edge when applying to jobs on USAJobs.gov. The information I found was scattered and confusing, but I slowly started to piece it together. It took me several weeks to wrap my head around the hiring process and months later before I even realized the OPM Job Series handbook existed and that I should read it. I still struggled with the component of the federal hiring process that almost everyone struggles with, and that is the federal resume.

My first federal resume was lacking the necessary information; it was too vague and way too short. I had a 20-year Army career, but the experience wasn't being communicated in the right way. I had won leadership medals, awards, commendations, badges, and certificates during my time in the U.S. Army, but none of it mattered to anyone in the HR office. I knew exactly what I had done, and I could easily talk about it in conversation, but none of the Human Resource Specialists could give me maximum credit for any of my achievements, so my job applications didn't get referred, I didn't get invited to any interviews, and I didn't get any job offers. As the rejections started to pile up, I counted over a hundred not-referred and not-eligible emails; I knew that something had to change. If I kept doing the same thing, I would keep getting the same negative results.

I started to reach out to people I served with in the military who were now in federal government jobs. I politely asked for their resume. Some people never responded back to me, and others didn't feel comfortable sharing their resumes with me, but a couple of people did, and what I saw surprised me. The federal resumes that were successful had an incredible amount of detail. Actions that I thought were implied, such as "Responding to emails using Microsoft Outlook," were completely spelled out. I made the adjustments but still had limited success. I decided to start reaching out to more people about the federal hiring process, and then I learned the concept of targeting specific job series. Before this, I had been using USAJobs.gov like I would a Google search engine. I was typing random words that I thought I could do, such as "Administrative Specialist," and then clicking the search button. Or I would just randomly scroll through USAJobs.gov thinking to myself, "Yeah, I think I could do that job," maybe I should apply. I then realized that I was qualified for multiple job series, and for each job series, I should have a dedicated federal resume targeting it.

The next change I made was in the frequency of my job applications. I started applying a minimum of four times a day, which means that some days, I applied to different job series. The volume of applications started to result in dozens of referrals. This is an example of the phrase, "Start fast and break things." Instead of waiting until everything was perfectly lined up, I took the approach of "applying in volume" and making small adjustments along the way. Once I had a strong resume and focused on a few different job series, I started applying in volume, and it only took a couple of months before I had multiple interview requests. The first one was the Department of Transportation, and I thought the interview went amazing. I drove three hours from North Carolina to Washington, D.C., to attend the interview in person. I knew I had given a wonderful performance, and everyone smiled at the end and shook my hand, so imagine my surprise when I learned a week later they had selected another person for the job. I was so sure of my performance after the interview that I completely stopped applying to jobs the week I was waiting for the results. It was then that I promised myself I would never stop applying until I was working at my desk on my first day of work.

I continued to go on interviews with the Department of Veterans Affairs, the Department of Labor, the Federal Emergency Management Agency, and the Department of Homeland Security, among other agencies. Then, I started to get job offers. The first job offer came from Veterans Affairs, and it was for a GS-13 Management Analyst position. I accepted and during my first week at the VA's Headquarters in Washington D.C. I received an email from the

Department of Homeland Security offering me a GS-14 job. I immediately agreed and was excited about the instant promotion. What I learned in the coming weeks is that I wouldn't be able to accept that job. The reason why was that I had used VEOA to accept the GS-13 position, and the GS-14 job was not an "open to the public" job, so I would be constrained by time-in-grade rules. In the government's eyes, I only had 7 days as a GS-13, and I needed 12 months to satisfy the time-in-grade rules. If the GS-14 job offer was an "open to the public" job, then there would have been no problem, but that wasn't the case.

For the next year, I knew that I was capable of a GS-14 job, but I accepted the first job offer that came my way because I was anxious and nervous about leaving the Army and craved stability for my family. I waited twelve months while working the GS-13 job and as soon as I reached the one-year mark, I aggressively started my job-searching campaign once again. This time, everything went smoother. It didn't take me long to start getting interviews at different federal agencies, and then a few months later, I received and accepted my GS-14 job offer. I did feel some guilt about leaving my first federal agency after such a short period of time, but I knew the higher-paying job would improve my life, and I gave six weeks of notice and left on friendly terms.

The reason the hiring process went so quickly the second time was not because I knew more government insiders but because I was now very familiar with writing federal resumes, the power of volume, and the entire hiring process. Friends of mine started to ask me to review their resumes, but despite my explanations, they still would not change their resumes, and they still would not apply in volume. I was spending so much time helping people that I decided maybe I would try to make a video on YouTube. If anyone asked me questions about government jobs, I could just point them to the video instead of spending the time explaining it again. This started out with an explanation of the GS Pay Scale, but I continued to make videos, and it has been an incredible journey. The reach I was able to have with a video has far exceeded anything I could have imagined, and the YouTube Channel has now crossed over 2,000,000 views in total, which is a number I can't wrap my head around.

As of writing this, I am still happily working in a federal government job. The work/life balance of my position allows me to pursue other projects and has given me the time to start my YouTube channel and write this book. I am not sure if I will be quitting anytime soon, but I do know that I still want to help people navigate toward their job offers. I have been hosting a live stream on YouTube, answering federal government job questions every month, and you are more than welcome to join me with any questions you may have. The main obstacle I see people continuing to have is writing their resume in a way that demonstrates they are not just "qualified" but "best qualified" and identifying the right job series that aligns with their unique experiences.

There is a segment of the U.S. population that looks at the public sector with a negative lens. They believe that the federal government is too big and that we should not be spending tax revenue on employing even more federal workers. They do not see the benefit of what the government can do on a day-to-day basis. To many of these people, there is no convincing them otherwise, but I strongly believe that there are many important functions our government does that dramatically improve people's lives all over the country, and many federal employees have a deep sense of service and duty. They have valuable skills and abilities, and they want to improve our country. It is important that the government is able to select top talent from multiple industries to continue serving the public.

I strongly believe that federal government jobs make up the core of the U.S. middle class, and public sector jobs are one of the last jobs that still guarantee a strong benefits package to its employees. It enables you to have the money to provide for yourself and others while serving the American public. It also gives you time back in your life through work/life balance and work flexibility. There are amazing developmental positions, and I think it's still one of the best-kept secrets that many people do not talk about and do not consider. Many people automatically think the pay is too low, which is often incorrect, and many people do not even consider it a real employment option. I'm glad you have decided it is a worthy challenge, and I wish you the best in your government job journey.

YOUR QUESTIONS

Over the past several years, I have received thousands of questions about the federal hiring process. I don't always know the answers, so that forces me to research them or ask other people who know the answers. Many of these questions could probably be on your mind. Below are the answers to the top twenty questions that I have been asked.

1. Should I submit a Cover Letter in my Job Application?

    No. Usually, I would not recommend attaching a cover letter to a job application. The only exception is if a cover letter is specifically mentioned in the "Required Documents" section of the job announcement. The hiring manager will probably already have over a hundred pages to review, and most people do not want to read an additional page that was not required.

2. If I accept a government job with a lower GS grade and start working, can I accept a higher GS grade offer?

    Yes, but it will depend. When applying to "open to the public" job announcements, the time-in-grade rules do not apply. So, if you are using your past experience to qualify for the job, then your ple, there is no convincing them otherwise, but I strongly believe that there are many important functions our government does that dramatically improve people's lives all over the country, and many federal employees have a deep sense of service and duty. They have valuable skills and abilities, and they want to improve our country. It is important that the government is able to select top talent from multiple industries to continue serving the public.

I strongly believe that federal government jobs make up the core of the U.S. middle class, and public sector jobs are one of the last jobs that still guarantee a strong benefits package to its employees. It enables you to have the money to provide for yourself and others while serving the American public. It also gives you time back in your life through work/life balance and work flexibility. There are amazing developmental positions, and I think it's still one of the best-kept secrets that many people do not talk about and do not consider. Many people automatically think the pay is too low, which is often incorrect, and many people do not even consider it a real employment option. I'm glad you have decided it is a worthy challenge, and I wish you the best in your government job journey.

YOUR QUESTIONS

Over the past several years, I have received thousands of questions about the federal hiring process. I don't always know the answers, so that forces me to research them or ask other people who know the answers. Many of these questions could probably be on your mind. Below are the answers to the top twenty questions that I have been asked.

1. Should I submit a Cover Letter in my Job Application?

    No. Usually, I would not recommend attaching a cover letter to a job application. The only exception is if a cover letter is specifically mentioned in the "Required Documents" section of the job announcement. The hiring manager will probably already have over a hundred pages to review, and most people do not want to read an additional page that was not required.

2. If I accept a government job with a lower GS grade and start working, can I accept a higher GS grade offer?

    Yes, but it will depend. When applying to "open to the public" job announcements, the time-in-grade rules do not apply. So, if you are using your past experience to qualify for the job, then your current government position will not matter. But if you accept a government job using VEOA and the other job you applied to was not "open to the public," then you would be bound by time-in-grade rules and would not be able to accept it.

I often recommend people accept multiple job offers because you never know when one might be rescinded. Also, do not feel guilty quitting your current job to accept a better job offer. This happens daily in the federal government, and Human Resource Offices and hiring managers understand that you have to do what is in your best interest when accepting a job offer.

3. **I keep getting referred, but I have not gotten an interview yet; why?**

    The reason you are not getting interviews is that the hiring manager is looking at your resume and actively deciding not to interview you. The best thing you can do is improve your resume and make your achievements more compelling and relevant to give the hiring manager a strong reason to want to interview you. Getting referred to the hiring manager is a good indicator, and in some cases, you just need to keep applying.

4. **Why does it take so long to get a government job?**

    The main reason it takes four to six months is because the government does not operate on profits, and it does not have a strong incentive to move fast, such as the private sector. Also, consider that everyone in the hiring process has multiple additional responsibilities aside from hiring you. The obstacles are: 1. The Human Resource Specialist, 2. The Hiring Manager, and 3. The Security Team. If any of those people take leave or have a large workload, then it could add even more time to the hiring process.

5. Do you have to know someone on the inside?

No. This is a common misconception. Although, plenty of people are able to leverage their existing connections to make getting a federal government job easier. More people are able to get a government job on their own merit, and it is still completely possible to apply, interview, and secure a government job offer without knowing a single person in the federal government. Do not get discouraged by people who say you have to know someone on the inside.

6. Why do veterans get all the government jobs?

They don't. It might seem like Veterans have it easy with federal government jobs, but the truth is they struggle just like everyone else. 75% of federal employees are not veterans. However, the hiring system does give them an advantage, but if they do not have the right experience, they will not be getting hired for the job. Experience is paramount, and many veterans do not have the right experience or do not know how to communicate their experience on their resumes. If you do not want to compete with veterans' preference, then consider targeting the job announcements under "direct hiring authority" as they do not consider veterans' preference at all.

7. Am I too old for a government job? Does ageism exist?

There are some jobs, such as special agent, air traffic controller, correctional officer, and police officer, where there is an actual age limit, usually 37 years old or 40 years old, with a waiver. But in the majority of government jobs, there is no age limit. I have seen people hired into the federal government in their late sixties. However, ageism exists everywhere and will continue to exist despite whatever policies or laws are passed. The average age of a federal employee, which is 47 years old, is a lot older than the average age of a private sector employee. I believe, overall, you will experience a lot less ageism in the federal government.

8. Can I dispute the fact I didn't get referred?

Yes. If you receive an email explaining that you were not found eligible or not referred, you can contact the point of contact listed at the bottom of the job announcement and attach your resume with a clear explanation of your experience that is relevant to the job announcement and then ask to be reconsidered. HR Specialists are not perfect, and just like anyone else, they make mistakes sometimes. There are times when it will be too late, but then again, there are times when asking for reconsideration has resulted in an applicant receiving a referral.

9. When is the right time to contact HR about the hiring status?

The only time I would reach out to inquire about the hiring status is after you have completed the interview. If you were referred but not invited to interview, there is usually no benefit in reaching out. Instead, you should keep applying for other government jobs. If you have already interviewed, I would wait three weeks after the interview and then reach out to the person who scheduled the interview to ask for a status update.

10. Do you need a college degree to get a government job?

No. Most federal government jobs do not have an educational requirement at all. The part most people get confused about is when they read that to qualify under education for a government job at the GS-9 level, you need a master's degree, and to qualify under education for a GS-11, you need a Ph.D.

This does not mean you need a college degree to be a GS-9 or GS-11. You don't need any college at all if you have the relevant experience. If you have NO experience and a master's degree, then you could be eligible for a GS-9, but the person with relevant experience will usually be selected over someone with only a college degree and no experience.

11. How long does it take to hear back after being interviewed?

The time varies greatly depending on the federal agency. Usually, I see an average of between two and six weeks. You will normally be contacted before the agency checks your references. But do not wait idly by checking your email for the results; keep applying for other government jobs that you are eligible for. So many people freeze and make no progress when waiting to hear back from a federal agency.

12. Should I take a pay cut to get into the government?

Maybe. This depends on your financial situation and goals. I normally urge people not to take a pay cut because there is this idea of "getting your foot in the door" that I do not agree with. If you are an experienced professional with 10+ years of proven relevant experience, then the only reason to take a pay cut is because there are no decent-paying jobs in your location. The chances are you can leverage your past experience and come in at a higher GS grade. What I am strongly against is people who transition into the federal government with over 15 or 20 years of experience and then settle for a GS-6 or GS-7 because they thought they had to take a lower GS grade; that is completely false.

However, taking a pay cut might make sense if you want to take a step back to take two steps forward. This is by accepting a job with a promotional ladder. You can accept a GS-9 with the promotional potential of a GS-12 and then two years later be a GS-12, earning close to six figures a year.

13. Is a Thrift Savings Plan (TSP) the same as a 401k or Individual Retirement Account (IRA)?

It is similar as it allows you to invest in the financial markets. This is the main reason why there are thousands of TSP millionaires. The investment is matched up to 5% of your contributions, and you can experience exponential growth. One key difference is that you cannot invest in an individual stock as you might do with an IRA. There are five main funds that you can pick along with lifecycle funds, so it is not that customizable. Most people tend to select the C and S fund to get maximum exposure to the S&P 500 and Dow Jones U.S. Completion Total Stock Market Index. Make sure you check with a financial advisor before selecting your funds, but I highly suggest changing it from the default settings.

14. How long does it take to be eligible for the federal pension?

It only takes five years. The years do not have to be consecutive. You can do a couple of years now and then come back ten years from now and do the last three. All of the time will count toward your Service Computation Date (SCD). The longer you work for the federal government, the larger your monthly pension payments will be. But keep in mind that you are contributing 4.4% of your salary to your federal pension.

15. I already have a security clearance. Will I need another one?

Probably. A lot of federal agencies will want to reinvestigate you for one reason or another. The whole process seems counterintuitive, and it is time-consuming to fill out over a hundred pages for an SF86, which is the document to apply for a security clearance. This can happen when moving from active-duty military to the Department of Homeland Security or the Department of Justice. If you are changing federal agencies or coming from the military, I would be prepared to redo your clearance.

16. How soon before leaving the military can I apply?

You can apply whenever you want, but if you want to leverage "veterans preference," then you need a Statement of Service in place of your DD214.

It is a memo that S-1 can give you. It has the expected nature of your discharge, and it needs to be signed by your commander. This document can be used within 120 days of your separation. The big question is, does this mean when I go on terminal leave or when I am officially discharged? I think it could potentially mean both, depending on what date your commander is comfortable signing.

17. Should I use a resume writing service?

I do not think so. Instead, I would ask a current federal employee for their resume, and you can use the style, format, and achievement structure in your resume. A lot of resume writers do not truly specialize in federal resumes, and the ones that do tend to be very expensive. I believe that everyone considering federal employment has the ability to write a competitive resume, but they might be lacking an example (that's why I provided one in the book), or they might not have time to do it. Consider that even if you pay someone to write your resume, you will still have to be on the phone with them explaining all of your achievements, so it is still time-consuming. Try to write it yourself; you will improve your resume writing skills and save money.

18. Should I work in defense contracting before trying to get a government job?

You do not need to, but many people do. A clear benefit of working for a defense contractor is that you usually get to interact with federal employees, and then you can start becoming a known person. Also, in many cases, a defense contracting job can pay a higher salary, but there is no pension. Having a defense contracting job is not a requirement, and plenty of people are able to transition to the federal government successfully without working as contractors.

19. Is it easier to get back into the government if you were a federal employee?

It can be. If you work in the competitive service for three years or more, you will be considered a "status candidate," and you will be able to apply for federal government jobs under the competitive service for the rest of your life. This is a big advantage over the general public, who are limited in the hiring paths they can apply to. But it will not be quick or easy. You will still have to search and apply just like you did the first time. The federal hiring process will still take four to six months, regardless of whether you are a prior federal employee or not.

20. Which federal agency is the best to get into?

The answer is the National Aeronautics and Space Administration (NASA), as they have been ranked #1 for many years on the Best Places to Work website. If you are interested in seeing the annual federal agencies rankings that are categorized by agency size, then check out the list on this website: https://bestplacestowork.org/rankings/

ACKNOWLEDGMENTS

I would like to first thank my lovely wife, Mariela Curet, for supporting my efforts to write this book and for her belief in me. My deepest appreciation to my mother, Teresa Balderrama, whom I inherited my work ethic from, and my sister, Marjorie Curet, for their assistance, talks, and constant encouragement. And to my kids for bringing me joy and happiness on a daily basis. I would also like to thank everyone who has ever watched my videos and subscribed to my YouTube channel. So many people have taken the time to leave a kind comment, and it has served as motivation to continue to make videos and help many people attain meaningful and well-paying careers.

ABOUT THE AUTHOR

Armand Rene Curet was born in New Iberia, Louisiana, and completed twenty years of active duty in the U.S. Army from 1999 to 2019. During his time in the Army, he deployed for seven months to Kosovo to support a peacekeeping operation and three times to Iraq in support of Operation Iraqi Freedom for 36 months. He was awarded the Major General Aubrey "Red" Newman award for leadership, The Order of the Kentucky Colonels issued by the Governor of Kentucky, and the De Fleury Medal (Bronze) by the U.S. Army Engineer Association for rendering significant service to an element of the Army Engineer Regiment. He also served as a board member of the Historic Fairfax City Inc. He created a YouTube Channel that is focused on helping people get federal government jobs and on self-development topics that have over 2,000,000 million total views. He lives with his wife and kids in Virginia.

Follow me on LinkedIn:

https://www.linkedin.com/in/armandcuret/

Follow me on YouTube:

https://www.youtube.com/c/armandcuret1

www.ingramcontent.com/pod-product-compliance
Lightning Source LLC
LaVergne TN
LVHW051603080426
835510LV00020B/3115